Easy ESL Crossword Puzzles

Easy ESL Crossword Puzzles

Chris Gunn, Lanternfish ESL

New York Chicago San Francisco Athens London Madrid
Mexico City Milan New Delhi Singapore Sydney Toronto

1 2 3 4 5 6 7 8 9 10 11 12 13 14 15 16 17   RHR/RHR   1 0 9 8 7 6 5 4 3

ISBN   978-0-07-182134-6
MHID   0-07-182134-1

Interior design by THINK Book Works

McGraw-Hill Education products are available at special quantity discounts to use as premiums and sales promotions or for use in corporate training programs. To contact a representative, please visit the Contact Us pages at www.mhprofessional.com.

This book is printed on acid-free paper.

Contents

Introduction
Not Just Vocabulary Review

Crosswords are an entertaining and stimulating source of vocabulary review. The crosswords in this collection will test your knowledge of the definition and use of more than 3,000 words. But this collection is intended to provide much more than vocabulary review. These crosswords are also intended to provide structured input that will benefit ESL learners in a number of ways. You will

- be exposed to useful strategies for defining vocabulary items.
- gain a better awareness of collocations and fixed phrases.
- practice using context to grasp meaning and make predictions.
- gain a better sense of word play such as rhyme, alliteration, and simile.

Whether you are a student studying on your own or a teacher looking to supplement your lessons, these crosswords will be a valuable resource for language learning.

The 110 crosswords included here cover a wide variety of topics and language skills. The puzzles fall into six broad categories, each with its own features and learning goals. The categories are

 Word Skills

 It's All Relative

 Collocation Awareness

 Fixed Phrases

 All on a Theme

 Holidays and Celebrations

Word Skills and It's All Relative

One major design feature of these crosswords is strategies for discussing what a word or phrase means and providing students with countless examples of how these strategies can be applied to define a word. These strategies are vital for clearing up miscommunications that occur when someone doesn't understand a vocabulary item. These strategies include using synonyms, antonyms, categories, examples, noun modification, metalanguage, and, most important, relative clauses.

In the *Word Skills* crosswords, the first six strategies are used to create clues such as: **persuade**, *another word for convince*; **shallow**, *the opposite of deep*; **iguana**, *a type of lizard*; **blizzard**, *a heavy snowstorm*; and **geese**, *the plural form of goose*.

In *It's All Relative* crosswords, clues are created using only relative clauses. This definition strategy is a powerful tool for teacher and student alike. In this strategy, a definition is created by combining a category with a defining detail that distinguishes the word from other words in that category. The defining detail is attached to the category with a relative clause. Some examples of this kind of clue include the following: **mechanic**, *a person who fixes cars*; **library**, *a place where people borrow books*; **election**, *a time when people vote for their government*; and **shovel**, *a tool that people use to dig holes*.

The primary goal of these types of crosswords then is not mere vocabulary review. It is to provide learners with massive exposure to definition strategies with the hope that they will be able to better understand and apply these strategies when they need them.

Collocation Awareness and Fixed Phrases

Another important feature built into the design of these crosswords is collocation awareness. Roughly speaking, we say that two words are **collocations** if they occur frequently together. Because they do occur frequently together, their combination seems natural when heard. Often, what a language learner says seems awkward not because of poor grammar but because of poor word choice. The learner is using a combination of words that native speakers just don't normally use. That is to say, the learner has chosen the wrong collocation. In English, you *have* a snowball fight, not *play*, *make*, or *do* a snowball fight as you would in other languages. For producing natural, native-like language, knowing what company a word keeps is almost as important as knowing what it means. And so, many of the crosswords found here require learners to *pay* attention to surrounding context for collocation clues: What do you *set* before dinner? The verb *set* collocates with *table*.

Phrasal verbs are one structure where noticing collocations is very important. A phrasal verb, which is a combination of a verb plus a preposition or an adverb, has a very different meaning from the verb on its own. For example, the definition of *run* changes dramatically depending on what follows. If you *run into* someone at the store, you meet that person unexpectedly. However, if you *run out of* something, then you use it all up. In the phrasal verb crosswords, noticing the collocating preposition is essential for solving the puzzle, as in the following: **try**, *you should _____ that sweater **on** before you buy it.*

This phrasal verb example also demonstrates a third feature of these crosswords, which is how clues can be used to train students to use context to understand meaning. The terms *sweater* and *before you buy it* provide the context for trying something on. Many of the crosswords require students to utilize context to solve the clues: **alarm**, *set your _____ to wake up early* and **grab**, *I'm hungry. Let's _____ a bite to eat* are but two examples.

Along with collocation awareness, these crosswords also test learners' knowledge of **fixed phrases**. Much of what we say comes in the form of fixed phrases such as proverbs, idioms, and other lexical chunks. Fixed phrases include things like *on the other hand*, *the grass is always greener*, *light as a feather*, and *make up your mind*. Having a ready supply of fixed phrases can help learners create more fluent speech.

All on a Theme and Holidays and Celebrations

The crosswords under the headings *All on a Theme* and *Holidays and Celebrations* are examples of crosswords with review as the primary goal. However, all of the skills emphasized in the other puzzle types are built into the clues for these crosswords as well. The ten *Holidays and Celebrations* puzzles focus on North American holidays.

In short, these crosswords have been designed to be more than just vocabulary review. They are an attempt to provide students with valuable, structured input and help them become better language learners.

Helpful Tips

As you work through the puzzles, keep the following tips in mind.

1. Keep a word journal for new words and difficult clues. Many of the vocabulary items are repeated in later crosswords. Keeping track of difficult clues will help you later on.

2. Don't assume that because a word fits it must be the answer. The word must fit with all of the intersecting words in the grid as well. You may have to experiment with different combinations to solve the puzzle as a whole. Use a pencil so you can erase mistakes! **Note:** if you see something like (4,5) in a clue, that means that the answer is two words, where the first word has 4 letters and the second word has 5 letters. If numbers are hyphenated (4-4) then the answer is two words separated by a hyphen (ping-pong).

3. Pay attention to collocations such as surrounding verbs and prepositions. They will often give you vital clues.

4. There are often clues within the clues themselves. For example in the clue <have a lot to do: as _____ as a bee>, you can guess the answer is *busy* even if you have never heard the simile *as busy as a bee,* since *having a lot to do* means you are *busy.*

5. Look out for instances of word play such as alliteration or rhyme. Alliteration is a repetition of sounds at the beginning of words, such as *copycat, candy cane,* or *penny-pincher.* Rhyme is a repetition of sounds from the final vowel to the end of the word, such as *cook* and *book* or *great* and *hate.* Many fixed expressions in English become fixed expressions precisely because they contain word play. For example, if we are at a crucial moment, we can say it is *make or break, sink or swim,* and *do or die.* All of those expressions contain either alliteration or rhyme. The same goes for proverbs such as *look before you leap* and *haste makes waste.*

6. Most of all, have fun!

ACROSS

1. The antonym of best.
5. The antonym of mean (like a bully).
7. The opposite of windy.
8. The antonym of black.
10. The antonym of wet.
11. The antonym of real.
13. The antonym of stingy.
18. The opposite of cooked.
19. The antonym of light (as a feather).
21. The opposite of dark.
22. The antonym of spicy.
23. The antonym of dim.
26. The antonym of many.
28. The antonym of hardworking.
31. The antonym of tight.
32. The opposite of first.
33. The antonym of soft.
34. The opposite of cold.
35. The opposite of sad.

DOWN

2. The opposite of polite.
3. The opposite of true.
4. The antonym of rich.
6. The antonym of old.
7. The opposite of rare.
9. The opposite of thick.
10. The opposite of alike.
12. The antonym of smooth.
14. The opposite of late.
15. The antonym of crooked.
16. The opposite of worthless.
17. The antonym of deep.
20. The opposite of clean.
22. The opposite of tidy.
24. The opposite of sick.
25. The opposite of long.
26. The opposite of stale (as in stale bread).
27. The opposite of tame.
29. The opposite of humid.
30. The opposite of far.

2 The Weather

1. Another way to say cold.

3. Crystals of ice that fall from the sky.

4. Flashes of light in a stormy sky.

9. Small, hard balls of ice that fall from the sky.

12. Another word for wet.

13. Not sunny.

14. A light wind.

16. A light rain.

18. Something children make when it snows.

21. A cloud that sits on the ground.

22. A time when there is lots of wind and rain.

23. Water that falls from the sky.

24. Not a cloud in the sky: A _____ day.

25. A dangerous twisting column of air.

26. Any form of water that falls from the sky.

DOWN

1. The opposite of windy.

2. Good weather for flying kites.

3. Another way to say sunlight.

5. A very large and dangerous storm that brings strong winds and heavy rains.

6. The opposite of hot.

7. Noise that goes with lightning.

8. A time when too much rain causes rivers to overflow.

10. Something people use when it rains.

11. The opposite of wet.

14. A snowstorm.

15. A time when too little rain causes rivers to dry up and plants to die.

17. The temperature at which water freezes (in Celsius).

18. A piece of snow.

19. A short rain.

20. A piece of rain.

21. A prediction of future weather.

All on a Theme

ACROSS

3. A place where sick people are treated.

5. A place where you see historical artifacts.

7. A place where people see movies.

9. A place where children learn.

10. A place where you can see fish and other marine life.

12. A place where you can buy dogs, cats, fish, and hamsters: A _____ shop.

13. A place where people can go for walks.

14. A place where people board trains, subways, and intercity buses.

15. A place where people order food.

17. A place where people work out.

18. A place where people wait for the bus: A bus _____.

20. A place where criminals are kept.

21. A place where people park their cars: A parking _____.

22. A place where people can buy a variety of goods: A _____ store.

23. A place where people buy bread.

25. A place where cars can drive fast.

26. A place where many families live together in the same building.

DOWN

1. A place where people drink coffee.

2. A place where people can walk (next to the road).

4. A place where two roads meet.

6. A place where many shops are gathered under one roof: A shopping _____.

8. A place where people mail parcels and letters: A _____ office.

11. A place where adults learn.

12. A place where children play.

14. A place where people watch baseball or soccer.

16. A place where people board airplanes.

19. A place where people display works of art.

21. A place where people borrow books.

22. A place where boats and ships stay.

23. A place where people save their money.

24. A place where people drive cars.

25. A place where people live.

4 On a Calendar

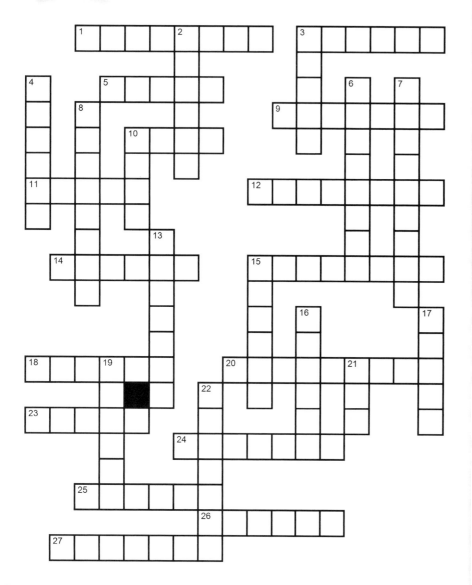

ACROSS

1. The day before Friday.

3. The first day of the workweek.

5. Day three of the month: The _____.

9. The month when people celebrate Halloween.

10. The first month of summer.

11. The month when people play tricks.

12. The month when people celebrate Christmas.

14. The last day of the workweek.

15. The first day of the weekend.

18. The season when snow covers the ground.

20. The month when many North Americans go back to school.

23. The number of days in a week.

24. Saturday and Sunday: The _____.

25. Day two of the month: The _____.

26. The last month of summer.

27. A time when people take time off and celebrate.

DOWN

2. The season when farmers plant crops.

3. The month when people celebrate St. Patrick's Day.

4. The day after Saturday.

6. The month when people celebrate Thanksgiving.

7. The day of the week that begins with W.

8. The month when people celebrate Valentine's Day.

10. The middle month of summer.

13. The first month of the year.

15. The season when families go to the beach.

16. The season when leaves change color.

17. Day one of the month: The _____.

19. The number of months in the year.

21. The fifth month of the year.

22. The day before Wednesday.

ACROSS

1. Go to the _____ to buy some bread.
2. Get a _____ to earn some money.
4. Go to the _____ to work out.
6. Stretch your _____ to prevent injury when you exercise.
7. Wear a _____ to protect your head.
11. Set your _____ to wake up early.
13. Use an _____ to withdraw some cash.
14. Put on some _____ to prevent dry skin.
15. Use a _____ to carry your cash.
17. Use a _____ to unlock a door.
18. Step on a _____ to check your weight.
19. Put on some _____ to keep your feet warm.
22. Call the _____ _____ to report a fire. (4,10)
27. Put a _____ on your hook to catch a fish.
28. Go on a _____ to lose some weight.
29. Call a _____ _____ to book your flight or plan a trip. (6, 5)
30. Mix yellow and _____ to make orange.

DOWN

1. Ride a _____ to cut down on gas consumption.
3. Mix yellow and _____ to make green.
5. Go to the _____ to see an exhibit.
7. Raise your _____ to ask a question.
8. Send an _____ to contact someone. (1-4)
9. Put on some _____ to keep your hands warm.
10. Check your _____ _____ to see how much money you have. (4,7)
12. Look through a _____ to see some cells.
15. Open a _____ to let some air in.
16. Look through a _____ to see the moons of Jupiter.
18. Wear a _____ to cut down on heat use.
20. Use some _____ to wash your hands.
21. Open the _____ to let someone in.
22. Use a _____ to organize your files.
23. Use a _____ to dry yourself off.
24. Dial a _____ to call someone.
25. Use a _____ to wipe the table.
26. Sit by the _____ to keep warm.

6 Colors, Numbers, Shapes

ACROSS

2. A mix of white and red.
3. A number that begins with O.
4. The color of snow.
6. The number of legs on an insect.
7. The color of the sky.
9. A number that means none.
10. A shape with two long sides and two short sides.
13. A round shape.
14. The color of leaves in spring.
16. A mix of red and yellow.
17. The number of months in a year.
18. The number of fingers on a hand.
19. The number of eyes on a face.
20. Three times three.
21. The number of days in a week.
22. The color of strawberries.

DOWN

1. The color of a banana.
2. A mix of red and blue.
5. A shape with three sides.
6. A shape with four equal sides.

7. The opposite of white.
8. The color of wood.
11. Five minus two.
12. A number that rhymes with wait.

15. Ten plus one.
16. A shape like an egg.
18. Three plus one.
19. The number of toes on two feet.

🔍 *All on a Theme*

ACROSS

2. The plural form of fungus.
4. The plural form of tooth.
5. The plural form of foot.
6. The plural form of fly.
8. The plural form of zero.
11. The plural form of wish.
12. The plural form of person.
15. The plural form of elf.
17. The plural form of tomato.
18. The plural form of tax.
19. The plural form of bus.
22. The plural form of berry.
24. The plural form of echo.
26. The plural form of witch.
28. The plural form of spy.
29. The plural form of child.

DOWN

1. The plural form of leaf.
3. The plural form of goose.
4. The plural form of that.
6. The plural form of fox.
7. The plural form of dish.
9. The plural form of reply.
10. The plural form of dress.
11. The plural form of woman.
13. The plural form of potato.
14. The plural form of hero.
16. The plural form of story.
19. The plural form of bench.
20. The plural form of mouse.
21. The plural form of this.
23. The plural form of loaf.
25. The plural form of cactus.
27. The plural form of man.

8 In a House

1. The top of a room.

3. A room where people sleep.

7. The part of a house that keeps the house dry when it rains.

10. An appliance used to dry clothes.

11. An appliance people use to cook food.

14. Something people turn on to see better when it's dark.

15. A place where people put books.

18. A room where people prepare food.

19. A piece of furniture on which people sleep.

20. A piece of furniture on which people write.

21. Something people flush.

25. A place where people keep dishes and food.

28. A comfortable place where more than one person can sit.

30. An appliance people watch for entertainment.

31. A place where people bake things.

32. Something people hang on their wall to decorate their house.

33. A place inside which people park their cars.

DOWN

1. Something people use to cover their windows.

2. A place where people grow flowers and plants.

4. Something people open to enter a room.

5. Something people use to see themselves.

6. A place to hang clothes.

8. A place where people burn wood for heat.

9. Part of a house that is underground.

12. Something you go up or down to get to another floor.

13. Something people hang on the wall to show the time.

16. An appliance used to keep food cool. (Casual form.)

17. Something people look through to see outside.

19. A room where people wash.

22. A piece of furniture on which people eat.

23. A piece of furniture on which people sit.

24. A flat place in a kitchen where people can put things and prepare food.

25. Another word for rug.

26. A room where people eat: _____ room.

27. An appliance used to keep food frozen.

29. Grassy space in front and back of a house.

All on a Theme

ACROSS

3. A person who fixes sinks, toilets, and pipes.

5. Someone who designs clothes: A _____ designer.

6. A person who cuts hair.

10. Somebody who designs buildings.

12. Somebody who delivers mail: A mail _____ .

14. A person who fixes wires in your house.

16. A person who performs experiments.

21. Somebody who fixes teeth.

23. Somebody who shows people around tourist sites: A tour _____ .

24. A person who cooks food (in a fancy restaurant).

26. Someone who drives a truck: A truck _____ .

27. A person who books airline tickets and hotels for you: A travel _____ .

DOWN

1. Someone who fixes cars.

2. Somebody who plays sports.

3. A person who makes computer programs.

4. Somebody who builds houses: A _____ worker.

5. Somebody who puts out fires.

7. A person who tells you the news.

8. Someone who catches criminals: A police _____ .

9. Somebody who grows crops.

11. Somebody who teaches children.

13. A person who acts in movies.

15. Someone who draws or paints pictures.

16. A person who sings songs.

17. Somebody who helps passengers on an airplane: A _____ attendant.

18. Someone who cleans buildings.

19. Someone who bakes bread.

20. Someone who helps sick people.

22. A person who helps doctors.

25. Someone who helps sick animals. (Casual form.)

It's All Relative

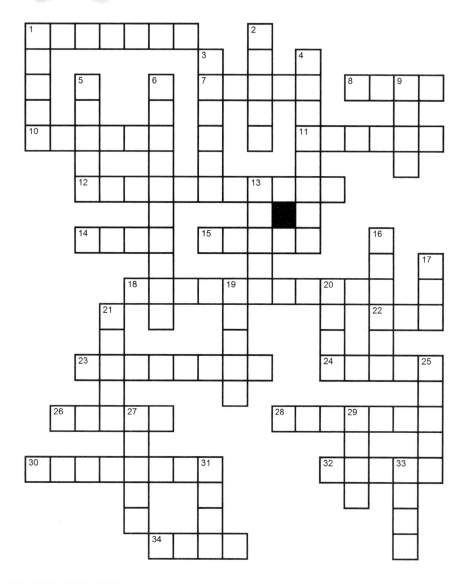

1. Spring saying: April showers bring May _____.

7. A spring month that begins with A.

8. Something birds build.

10. A plant that has just emerged from the soil.

11. A short rain.

12. In spring, many animals such as bears come out of _____.

14. Something kids decorate on Easter.

15. In spring, snow _____ in the mountains.

18. A butterfly larva.

22. A spring month that begins with M.

23. A spring flower that begins with D.

24. In spring, many _____ return from their wintering grounds.

26. Baby birds _____ from eggs.

28. A baby frog.

30. A time to wear green: St. _____ Day.

32. The part of a plant that takes in water from the earth.

34. A baby cow.

DOWN

1. A time for tricks: April _____ Day.

2. The first month of spring.

3. A place where people grow flowers and plants.

4. Something to see in spring: Cherry _____.

5. April 22nd: _____ Day.

6. A day to say thanks to mom.

9. The part of a plant that holds the leaves up.

13. A spring flower that begins with T.

16. A person who grows crops.

17. Birds _____ eggs in their nests.

19. A bird with a red breast.

20. A baby sheep.

21. _____ a tree on Arbor Day.

25. Something farmers plant to grow new crops.

27. A baby bird.

29. A tool that farmers use to break up the soil.

31. Another word for dirt.

33. In spring, the frozen ground begins to _____.

🔍 All on a Theme

ACROSS

4. Circle, square, or triangle.
5. Desks, tables, and beds.
6. Two, four, or eleven.
8. Ham, steak, or chicken.
10. Daisy, tulip, or daffodil.
13. Baseball, soccer, or hockey.
14. Bee, ant, or grasshopper.
15. Pianist, violinist, or guitarist.
17. Everest, Fuji, or Kilimanjaro.
18. Chess, checkers, or Monopoly.
20. Painter, sculptor, or illustrator.
21. Germany, Japan, or India.
22. Axe, saw, or shovel.
24. Walnut, pistachio, or pecan.
26. Pine, oak, or maple.
27. Owl, seagull, or parrot.
28. Brain, lungs, or stomach.
29. Carrot, onion, or lettuce.

DOWN

1. Bananas, oranges, or apples.
2. February, June, or July.
3. Madrid, Beijing, or Moscow.
4. Taste, touch, or hearing.
7. Emperor, pharaoh, or king.
8. Magazines, television, and newspapers.
9. Australia, Asia, or North America.
11. Amazon, Nile, or Mississippi.
12. Snake, turtle, or lizard.
13. Astronomer, biologist, or paleontologist.
15. Human, whale, or bat.
16. Blueberry, strawberry, or raspberry.
19. Ogre, skeleton, or vampire.
23. Pacific, Arctic, or Indian.
24. Prince, duke, or baron.
25. Basil, oregano, or pepper.

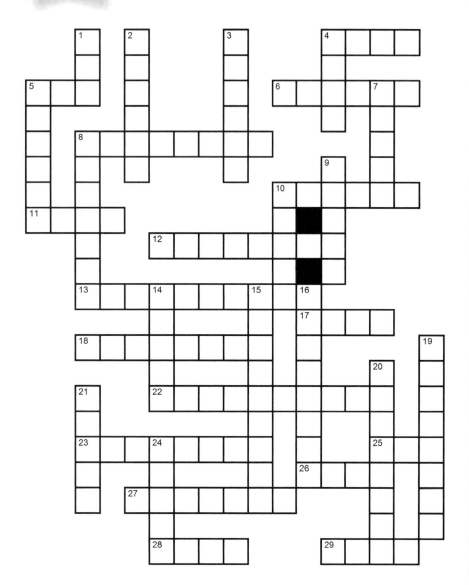

ACROSS

4. A place to go for walks.
5. Darker skin color from being in the sun.
6. Something you wear instead of pants.
8. You can cool off by _____ in the lake.
10. Something children collect at the beach.
11. Something that comes in and out at the beach.
12. A place where families have a barbecue.
13. Something people wear to protect their eyes from the glaring sun.
17. A period of very hot weather: A heat _____.
18. A time when kids don't go to school.
22. Something kids make at the beach.
23. An event where you cook hamburgers and hot dogs in summer.
25. Avoid the heat: Cool _____.
26. _____ on the air conditioner.
27. Sleeping in a tent in the outdoors.
28. Summer is a good time to go for a _____ in the mountains.
29. Avoid the heat: _____ cool.

DOWN

1. Something people use to stay cool.
2. Pack up some food and go somewhere outside to eat.
3. Something women wear at the beach.
4. A place where people go swimming.
5. Casual clothing you wear over your upper body in summer. (1-5)
7. Something you use to dry off.
8. Something you wear on your feet at the beach.
9. In summer, you have to pull _____ from the garden.
10. Rest under the _____ of a big tree.
14. In summer, you have to cut or mow the _____.
15. Something people put on their skin to prevent sunburn.
16. Something you wear when you go swimming.
19. Without shoes on.
20. A refreshing, sour beverage served in summer.
21. Something people put in drinks to keep them cold: Ice _____.
24. A sandy place next to the ocean.

🔍 *All on a Theme*

ACROSS

2. _____ away your toys.

5. _____ the doors before you go to bed.

7. _____ the garden to get rid of unwanted plants.

9. _____ the laundry out to dry.

11. _____ some errands.

12. _____ clothes so that they don't have any wrinkles.

13. _____ the mailbox to see if any mail has arrived.

16. _____ the windows to let some air in.

17. _____ the floor with a broom.

19. _____ the dishes after dinner.

21. _____ the flowers when the soil is dry.

23. _____ the rugs.

24. _____ your bed after you've slept in it.

25. _____ the laundry.

26. _____ the dog for a walk.

Chores 13

DOWN

1. _____ the table before dinner.

2. _____ up the things on the floor.

3. _____ the leaves in autumn.

4. _____ the laundry after it's dry.

6. _____ up a dirty room.

8. _____ off the lights.

10. _____ the dog a bath.

13. _____ some wood for the fire.

14. _____ the lawn.

15. _____ cans, glass, and newspaper.

17. _____ the driveway after it snows.

18. _____ the laundry into whites and colors.

20. _____ off the bookshelves.

21. _____ the table after dinner.

22. _____ up a messy room.

Collocation Awareness 🔗

13

1. A thing that changes color in autumn.
3. A yellow vegetable that grows on tall stalks.
4. _____ apples from the tree.
6. A fish that returns from the oceans to the rivers to lay eggs.
8. Ready to eat (as in a fruit or vegetable).
9. A yellow oval fruit that is common in fall.
13. Birds that fly south in the shape of a V.
14. A black bird that is infamous for stealing crops.
17. A holiday where children dress in costume to get candy.
19. Dry grass that is used to feed farm animals.
20. An autumn nut that many people roast.
23. The nut of an oak tree.
24. The last month of fall.
28. A tree that is famous for its red foliage.
29. A Halloween greeting: Trick or _____!
30. What farmers grow.
31. A fall color that rhymes with bed.
32. A large yellow flower on a tall stem.
34. A tool that people use to gather leaves.

2. Another way to say leaves.
3. _____ wood for the fire.
5. Children _____ jack-o'-lanterns for Halloween.
6. The first month of fall.
7. A fall color that begins with Y.
10. A bird that many Americans eat on Thanksgiving.
11. A thing that farmers use to guard the crops.
12. Leaves _____ to the ground.
15. Another word for collect.
16. Something children wear on Halloween.
18. Another word for fall.
21. _____ a pumpkin pie.
22. The plural form of leaf.
25. The middle month of fall.
26. A fall color that rhymes with town.
27. A red fruit that is common in fall.
29. Maple leaves _____ red.
33. A tree that begins with O.

🔍 All on a Theme

ACROSS

2. There's no such thing as a free _____.

4. Practice what you _____.

7. You can't teach an old _____ new tricks.

9. The _____ cannot change its spots.

10. Beauty is only _____ deep.

13. Many _____ make light work.

14. _____ is the spice of life.

15. Don't put the _____ before the horse.

16. Easy come, easy _____.

17. _____ makes the heart grow fonder.

21. A watched _____ never boils.

22. Birds of a _____ flock together.

25. _____ only knocks once.

28. The more the _____.

29. One man's meat is another man's _____.

31. Out of _____, out of mind.

32. Money is the root of all _____.

33. Let sleeping _____ lie.

34. Don't _____ the hand that feeds you.

DOWN

1. A poor workman always blames his _____.

2. Look before you _____.

3. Make _____ while the sun shines.

5. Don't put all your _____ in one basket.

6. _____ makes perfect.

7. Rome wasn't built in a _____.

8. _____ is twenty-twenty.

11. _____ is better than cure.

12. Good things come to those who _____.

13. If you can't take the _____, get out of the kitchen.

18. Talk is _____.

19. _____ is a dish best served cold.

20. Don't rock the _____.

21. A _____ paints a thousand words.

23. Walls have _____.

24. One good turn _____ another.

26. When it _____, it pours.

27. The squeaky _____ gets the grease.

28. _____ is right.

29. No _____, no gain.

30. Better _____ than sorry.

Fixed Phrases

16 Winter

1. In winter, people _____ down mountain slopes.
3. Ice that forms on windows or grass during the night.
5. Ten degrees below zero: _____ ten.
7. Something people wear over their shirts to keep warm in winter.
8. A piece of ice that hangs from your roof.
9. Stay warm by the _____.
11. In winter, the temperature _____. Hint: It begins with D.
13. A winter month that begins with F.
14. A winter team sport played on ice.
16. A shape children make by lying on the ground and flapping their arms: A snow _____.
18. Something people wear to keep their ears warm.
20. Children like to _____ snowball fights.
22. A winter drink: Hot _____.
23. People _____ the New Year on January 1st.
25. The temperature at which water freezes (in Celsius).
28. A promise people make on New Year's Day.
29. Something you ride down a snowy hill.

DOWN

1. Something you wrap around your neck to keep warm in winter.
2. The last month of the year.
4. People _____ on ice.
5. Children _____ snowmen.
6. People fall down on the ice because ice is _____.
7. A piece of snow.
10. Something you put on when you go outside in winter.
12. Something you wear instead of shoes in winter.
15. Something you wear on your hands in winter.
17. Change from water to ice.
19. An alternative to skis.
20. In winter, many animals _____ until spring.
21. A snowstorm.
23. Frost _____ the window.
24. Children _____ snowballs.
26. Come in from the _____ and get warm!
27. In winter, _____ covers the pond.

🔍 All on a Theme

ACROSS

1. A slow-moving mollusk that carries a shell on its back.
2. A bird raised for eggs.
4. A forest animal that has antlers.
6. A small primate that lives in trees and eats bananas.
8. A pet that has whiskers.
9. An insect that makes honey.
10. A large, ocean fish that has rows of sharp teeth.
14. A flightless bird that lives in Antarctica.
15. A large mammal that has a long neck and lives in Africa.
17. A farm animal that is raised for pork.
18. A venomous animal that lives in the desert.
20. A pet that people use to guard their homes.
22. An insect that drinks blood and spreads disease.
23. A striped animal that looks like a horse.
25. A dangerous reptile that has a long mouth and strong jaws.
26. A long-eared mammal with a small fluffy tail.
28. A ferocious mammal that has a mane and lives in Africa.
29. A reptile that carries a shell on its back.
30. A long, flying insect that catches mosquitoes.
32. A forest animal that hunts in packs.

DOWN

1. A long reptile that does not have any legs.
2. A domesticated animal that people keep for milk.
3. A large mammal that people ride through the desert.
4. A bird that is often found in wetlands.
5. A marine mollusk that sometimes makes pearls.
7. An Australian animal that is known for its ability to jump far.

9. A large omnivorous mammal that lives in the forest.
11. A large mammal with a long trunk and tusks.
12. A ferocious animal that has black and orange stripes.
13. A farm animal that people raise for wool.
16. A small forest animal that sometimes sneaks into the henhouse.
18. An eight-legged bug that makes a web.

19. A forest animal that gathers nuts for the winter.
21. A large primate that lives in Africa.
24. A mammal that can fly.
27. An insect that lives in a colony.
31. A bird that is active at night.

ACROSS

1. Server: _____ you like anything to drink with that?
2. What soup is served in.
5. A piece of beef that you can have cooked rare, medium, or well done.
7. A dish that consists of mixed vegetables chopped up.
8. Say that you will pay: It's my _____ .
11. Say that you will pay: It's _____ me.
12. A type of restaurant where you serve yourself.
13. Something people use to eat with in many Asian restaurants.
15. A utensil used to eat soup.
20. Cashier: Is that for _____ or to go?
21. Something you make to get a table in a busy restaurant.
22. The type of restaurant where you might find noodles, rice, and fortune cookies.
24. Server: May I _____ your order?
25. Something you eat before the main course.
27. An Italian dish that consists of noodles and tomato sauce.
29. What your food is served on.
30. What coffee is served in.

DOWN

1. Sign at the entrance: Please _____ to be seated.
2. The amount of money you have to pay for eating at a restaurant.
3. The type of restaurant where you might find sushi rolls.
4. Hamburgers, pizza, or french fries. (4,4)
6. I'm hungry. Let's _____ a bite to eat.
9. A utensil used to eat salad.
10. A utensil used to cut meat.
14. Server: Are you ready to _____ ?
15. A dish that consists of raw fish on top of rice.
16. A treat you have after your meal.
17. A thing that lists the food and prices at a restaurant.
18. The type of restaurant where you might find tacos and burritos.
19. A person who serves food in a restaurant.
22. A person who cooks at a fancy restaurant. Hint: It ends with F.
23. An Italian dish that is served by the slice.
26. A dish that consists of noodles and a sauce (like spaghetti or lasagna).
28. Extra money you give for good service.

Q **All on a Theme**

ACROSS

1. A farm animal that begins with G.
4. A month that ends with Y.
5. A shape that begins with C.
6. A piece of furniture that begins with T.
7. An ocean that begins with P.
8. A part of your hand that ends with B.
10. A fruit that begins with A.
13. A continent that begins with E.
15. A human organ that begins with L.
17. A forest animal that ends with X.
22. A tool that begins with SH.
23. A form of transportation that begins with T.
25. An insect that begins with G.
28. A tree that begins with P.
29. A piece of furniture that begins with CH.
31. A season that begins with W.
32. A tree that begins with O.
33. A vegetable that begins with C.
35. A flower that begins with T.

DOWN

2. A continent that begins with A.
3. A vegetable that begins with L.
4. A drink that begins with M.
5. A hot drink that begins with C.
7. A nut that begins with P.
9. A type of meat that begins with B.
11. A farm animal that begins with P.
12. A number that ends with X.
14. A marine animal that begins with O.
16. A season that ends with NG.
18. A bird that begins with O.
19. A color that ends with W.
20. A school subject that begins with M.
21. A hot drink that begins with T.
22. A shape that begins with S.
24. A metal that begins with I.
26. A bird that begins with P.
27. A bird that begins with C.
28. A color that ends with K.
30. A month that begins with A.
34. An insect that begins with A.

At the Movies

1. A popular movie snack.
8. Another word for theater.
10. A person who acts in movies.
11. A person who tells actors where to go and what to do.
12. A place where people watch movies.
15. The time and place of a movie.
16. A summary of a movie.
18. A person in a story or a movie.
20. The text that tells you who helped to make the movie.
21. The exciting finish of a movie.
24. Movies about robots, spaceships, and the future. (7,7)
27. A love story.
28. Part II of a movie.
29. Actors _____ roles in movies.
30. The part an actor plays. Hint: It begins with R.

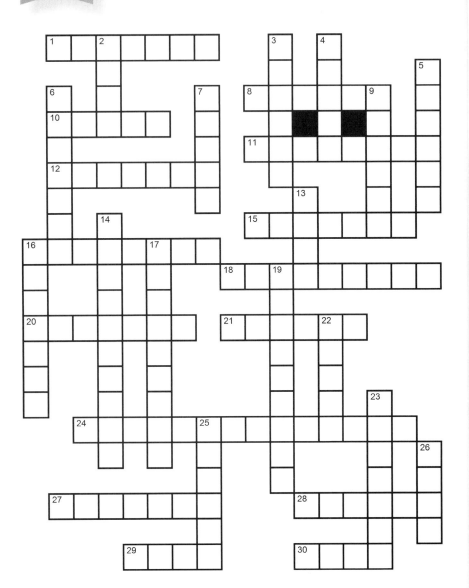

DOWN

2. What happens in a movie.
3. A person who says whether a movie was good or bad.
4. Part of a movie.
5. Kind of movie that makes you afraid.
6. Movies about dragons, knights, and wizards.
7. The type of movie.

9. Kind of movie with lots of fighting and explosions.
13. The lead actor.
14. The music in a movie.
16. Explosions, lights, and car crashes: _____ effects.
17. Text that helps people understand foreign-language films.

19. A movie that is created using cartoon characters or computer graphics.
22. This movie is _____ a boy who . . .
23. Something that actors wear.
25. A movie that makes you laugh.
26. Another word for movie.

🔍 All on a Theme

ACROSS

1. An American breakfast: Bacon and _____.
4. What you put in coffee: Cream and _____.
6. What a sentry asks: Friend or _____?
7. Wild West poster: Wanted dead or _____.
8. Parts of an essay: Introduction and _____.
10. Across the country: From coast to _____.
11. Lines on a map: Latitude and _____.
12. Things that break bones: Sticks and _____.
15. Compromise: Give and _____.
16. An early human: Hunter and _____.
18. Things to write with: Pen and _____.
20. Hunting tools: Bow and _____.
21. The setting of a story: The time and _____.
22. The whole night: From dusk to _____.
26. Eating utensils: Knife and _____.
28. The whole time: From beginning to _____.
29. A coin toss: Heads or _____.
30. Nonstop: Night and _____.
31. A marriage vow: For better or for _____.

DOWN

1. Why something happened: Cause and _____.
2. Something good government has: Checks and _____.
3. Fight as hard as you can: Fight tooth and _____.
4. The whole day: From sunrise to _____.
5. A Halloween greeting: Trick or _____!
9. Weighing an argument: Listing the pros and _____.
11. A good way to finish: Save the best for _____.
13. Your whole body: From head to _____.
14. The whole universe: Heaven and _____.
16. Your whole life: From cradle to _____.
17. Sewing implements: Needle and _____.
18. A link in the food chain: Predator and _____.
19. Things on a restaurant table: Salt and _____.
23. An old photograph: Black-and-_____.
24. Parents: Mom and _____.
25. Over the whole Earth: From pole to _____.
27. In a safe place: Under lock and _____.

22 Food and Cooking

ACROSS

1. _____ your food by cooking it too long.
4. Meat that comes from pigs.
6. Hot like a chili pepper.
7. A watery dish that is served in a bowl.
9. _____ up the oven before you put something in it to cook.
10. Bananas, oranges, and grapes.
11. Fish, crabs, lobsters, and clams.
13. _____ some bacon in a pan.
15. A light dish between meals.
17. An evening meal.
18. A treat that you have after a meal.
21. A staple food in Central America.
22. Meat that comes from cattle.
26. Carrots, lettuce, and beans.
27. _____ some cheese for your sandwich.
29. A midday meal.
30. The opposite of cooked.
31. A bowl of mixed, chopped vegetables.
32. _____ some bread in an oven.
33. A place where you bake bread.
34. Taste like sugar.
35. _____ some water in a pot.
36. Meat that comes from birds like chickens or turkeys.

DOWN

2. A staple food in Asia.
3. Salmon or tuna.
4. Dishes such as spaghetti or lasagna.
5. Taste like a lemon.
6. Oregano, basil, and pepper.
8. _____ some juice into a cup.
11. The opposite of fresh (as in fresh bread).
12. Products that are made from milk, like cheese and yogurt.
13. A cold place where you put meat so it doesn't spoil.
14. The opposite of spicy.
16. A place where people cook food.
19. A place where you heat up pots and pans.
20. A morning meal.
23. Just baked.
24. White crystals that many people add to food for extra flavor.
25. Meat that is cooked all the way through. (4,4)
28. A breakfast food that you pour milk over.
34. _____ your coffee with a spoon when you add cream.

All on a Theme

ACROSS

1. Quite chilly: As _____ as ice.

3. Hahahahaha!: _____ like a hyena.

8. Not living: As _____ as a doornail.

9. A color in nature: As _____ as grass.

10. Have a mischievous smile: _____ like a Cheshire cat.

11. Very dark in color: As _____ as coal.

12. Very similar: Like two _____ in a pod.

16. Sneaky: As _____ as a fox.

18. Simple: As _____ as ABC.

20. A winter color: As _____ as snow.

24. Easy to notice: _____ _____ like a sore thumb. (5,3)

25. Nice to look at: As _____ as a picture.

26. Ill: As _____ as a dog.

27. Fast asleep: _____ like a light.

28. Quiet: As _____ as the grave.

30. Know what someone is thinking: _____ someone like a book.

32. Easy to lift: As _____ as a feather.

33. Die or quit something rapidly: _____ like flies.

34. Sob a lot: _____ like a baby.

DOWN

2. Can't hold water: _____ like a sieve.

4. Stay away from something: _____ something like the plague.

5. Very solid: As _____ as rock.

6. Quite happy and healthy: _____ like a million bucks.

7. Go straight to the bottom: _____ like a stone.

8. Can't touch the bottom: As _____ as the ocean.

11. Have a lot to do: As _____ as a bee.

13. Sluggish: As _____ as a snail.

14. Hard to wake up: _____ like a log.

15. Hard to grab: As _____ as an eel.

17. Won't change your mind: As _____ as a mule.

19. Go around quickly: _____ like wildfire.

21. Ancient: As _____ as the hills.

22. Squashed: As _____ as a pancake.

23. Very fast: As _____ as a wink.

24. Soft to touch: As _____ as silk.

26. Clever: As _____ as a tack.

29. Not much appetite: _____ like a bird.

31. Not damp at all: As _____ as a bone.

24 Fruits and Vegetables

ACROSS

3. A leafy green vegetable that ends in CH.
6. A fruit with a fuzzy skin.
7. A soft, fleshy fruit that has many seeds on the inside. Hint: It begins with M.
9. A leafy green vegetable used to make coleslaw.
11. A red fruit that begins with A.
13. Something used to make spaghetti sauce.
14. Small green seeds that come in a pod.
16. A green vegetable that looks like a little tree.
18. A long orange root vegetable.
19. A tropical fruit that is yellow on the inside and is often sliced into rings.
21. A staple crop in Central America.
23. Purple fruit that grows on vines.
26. A small round berry used in jams and pies.
28. A large orange vegetable that is carved on Halloween.
29. A fungus that is sometimes used in salads.

DOWN

1. A red fruit that has many tiny seeds on the outside.
2. A vegetable that looks like little white trees.
4. A staple crop that is often used to make flour for bread.
5. A long, crunchy, pale green vegetable.
8. A sour fruit.
9. A small red fruit that comes from a tree and has a large pit.
10. Small oval-shaped vegetables often in pods. Hint: They begin with B.
12. A root vegetable used to make french fries.
15. A root vegetable that can make you cry when you chop it up.
16. A long yellow fruit.
17. A fruit that is also a color.
18. A green vegetable used to make pickles.
20. A leafy vegetable used to make salads.
22. A staple crop in Asia.
23. A root vegetable with a strong flavor.
24. An oval yellow or green fruit that rhymes with hair.
25. An oddly shaped yellow vegetable that is related to a pumpkin.
27. A purple tree fruit with a large pit.

All on a Theme

Before, During, After | 25

ACROSS

2. _____ something up when you drop it.
4. _____ someone up when they are feeling down.
5. _____ on your pajamas before you go to bed.
7. _____ the window when it's stuffy inside.
9. _____ a question when you are confused.
10. _____ your hands after a performance.
12. _____ on a door before you open it.
14. _____ dressed after you wake up.
16. _____ a doctor when you are ill.
18. _____ your nose when you have a cold.
20. _____ something when you are hungry.
22. _____ to music while you work out.
23. _____ a suit when you go to a job interview.
25. _____ your feet when you are angry.
27. _____ your teeth after you eat.
28. _____ food when you go to a restaurant.
29. _____ your tickets before you enter the theater.
32. _____ the table before dinner.
33. _____ your bill after you eat.
34. _____ something after you lose it.

DOWN

1. _____ something when you are thirsty.
3. _____ something when it is dirty.
4. _____ your bags before you board a plane.
6. _____ your server when the service was good.
8. _____ your bed after you wake up.
10. _____ the police when you witness a crime.
11. _____ the phone when it rings.
13. _____ a sandcastle when you go to the beach.
15. _____ some medicine when you are sick.
17. _____ your hands before you eat.
18. _____ some money when you are broke.
19. _____ when it's your birthday.
21. _____ on clothing before you buy it.
24. _____ off the lights before you go to bed.
25. _____ your shoulders when you don't know something.
26. _____ the table with a cloth after dinner.
30. _____ in your homework after you complete it.
31. _____ hard before an exam.
32. _____ sorry when you accidentally hurt someone.

Collocation Awareness

25

26 Travel

4. The kind of ticket you buy when you are not coming back. (3-3)
6. A place where you board ships.
8. Another word for bags.
9. A place where you board a bus or a train.
10. A time when people don't have to work.
11. A sandy place next to the ocean.
13. A form of transportation that goes on tracks.
14. A hard, rectangular piece of luggage with a handle.
17. A ticket that is good for both ways: _____-trip.
18. Get ready to go: _____ your bags.
19. Food and drink delivered right to your room: Room _____.
20. A person who books tickets for you: A travel _____.
22. A popular place for vacations.
26. What you sleep in when you are camping: A sleeping _____.
27. A place where you board a flight.
29. _____ your identification at the ticket counter.
30. A piece of identification that you need to travel abroad.

DOWN

1. A place to swim in your hotel.
2. A time when kids don't go to school.
3. A holiday on a ship.
5. A document you need to enter a country.
7. The time when your flight leaves: _____ time.
11. A bag that you carry over your shoulders.

12. _____ your bags before you get onto a plane.
13. A place in which to sleep when you are camping.
14. Something you buy to remember your trip.
15. A place where people sleep while on vacation.
16. A place to buy souvenirs: _____ shop.

20. The time when your flight lands: _____ time.
21. A trip for newlyweds.
23. A form of transportation that goes over water.
24. A person who is traveling.
25. A ship that carries people from one place to another.
26. _____ your tickets in advance.
28. Another word for journey.

🔍 All on a Theme

ACROSS

2. The past tense of fall.
4. The past tense of see.
8. The past tense of shoot.
9. The past tense of shake.
10. The past tense of make.
12. The past tense of begin.
14. The past tense of write.
16. The past tense of throw.
17. The past tense of do.
21. The past tense of give.
22. The past tense of wake.
23. The past tense of wear.
25. The past tense of catch.
27. The past tense of drink.
29. The past tense of hide.
30. The past tense of sleep.
33. The past tense of grow.
36. The past tense of find.
37. The past tense of tell.
38. The past tense of bite.

DOWN

1. The past tense of choose.
3. The past tense of lose.
4. The past tense of speak.
5. The past tense of swim.
6. The past tense of mean.
7. The past tense of fight.
11. The past tense of drive.
12. The past tense of blow.
13. The past tense of get.
14. The past tense of win.
15. The past tense of bring.
17. The past tense of draw.
18. The past tense of steal.
19. The past tense of become.
20. The past tense of buy.
24. The past tense of run.
26. The past tense of have.
27. The past tense of dig.
28. The past tense of eat.
31. The past tense of leave.
32. The past tense of meet.
34. The past tense of ride.
35. The past tense of go.

Word Skills

3. A bruise around your eye. (5,3)

6. Words written on a card sent to hospitals: Get _____ soon.

8. A hole in your teeth.

9. Doctor's advice: Get some _____ .

11. Doctor: I need to _____ some tests to find out what's wrong.

12. Not in good physical condition: Out of _____ .

15. Another way to say "have an operation": Have _____ .

17. A person who assists a doctor.

18. A hiking injury: A _____ ankle.

19. A place where you can have your prescription filled.

25. A person who sees a doctor.

26. An injury caused by something sharp like a knife.

28. An eye doctor.

29. Another word for sick.

30. An injury caused by something sharp like a cat's claw.

31. Feeling better: Back on your _____ .

1. Something you take when you are sick.

2. A high body temperature.

3. Black or blue mark under your skin.

4. Cover your mouth when you _____ .

5. Something that makes you sneeze.

7. Get sick: Come _____ with something.

9. Many small red bumps on your skin.

10. A cold symptom: Have a _____ throat.

13. A piece of paper a doctor gives you so you can get medicine.

14. A pain in your head.

16. A cold symptom: Have a _____ nose.

18. A sign that you are sick.

20. A place where you go when you have a serious illness or an operation.

21. Someone who takes care of your teeth.

22. A common winter illness.

23. A person who cures sick people.

24. A place where you go to see a doctor.

26. _____ a cold.

27. _____ some medicine.

30. _____ a doctor when you are sick.

Q **All on a Theme**

ACROSS

2. Something people use to cut wooden boards.
3. Something people use to paint.
8. A thing that people use to separate solids and liquids.
9. A tool that people use to find the direction north.
11. Something that people use to enter a building.
12. A thing that people use to write.
14. Something people use to tie things.
16. A thing that people use to boil eggs.
18. Something people use to eat soup.
20. A thing that people use to see objects in space.
24. A tool that people use to chop wood.
26. A thing that farmers use to dig up earth before planting.
27. A thing that people use to see in their house at night.
28. Something people use to fix pencil mistakes.
29. Something people use to look up information.
33. A thing that people use to carry money around.
34. A thing people use to eat salad.
35. A tool that people use to gather leaves.

DOWN

1. A thing that people use to cut meat.
2. Something people use to cut paper.
3. A thing people use to sweep.
4. Something people use to hold their pants up.
5. Something people use to keep other people out of their yard.
6. Something people use to see very tiny objects.
7. A thing that people use to water their gardens.

10. A form of transportation people use to carry goods over water.
13. A thing people use to sew.
15. Something people use to stick things together.
17. A thing people use to make calls.
18. A tool people use to dig.
19. A thing that people use to catch butterflies.
21. Something people use to attach papers together.

22. Something people use to eat noodles.
23. A thing that people use to fix ripped paper.
25. A type of string that people use when they sew.
26. A thing that people use to fry eggs.
30. A thing that people use to dry themselves.
31. A thing that people use to draw straight lines.
32. Something people use fish.

1. Goalkeepers try to _____ shots.
4. A person who chooses the winner in sports like gymnastics.
7. A person who tells a team what to do.
10. A part of a basketball game.
11. Something you need to play tennis or badminton.
12. A person who plays sports.
16. Something the champions get to take home.
18. A place where soccer and baseball games are held.
20. A team sport in which players kick a ball.
24. The shape of a baseball field.
25. A person who loves to watch a sport.
26. A person who protects the net in soccer.
28. The person or team you play against.
31. A sport in which athletes hit a ball over a net using a racket.
32. To begin a match in volleyball or tennis, someone has to _____ the ball.

DOWN

2. A place where tennis matches and basketball games are played.
3. If you _____ your opponent, you win.
5. Something you use to catch a baseball.
6. The number of points that each team has.
8. A team sport played on ice.

9. A sport in which athletes throw a ball through a hoop.
13. A part of a soccer match.
14. Things that athletes need to play a sport.
15. Something the referee blows.
17. The best score or time.
19. A part of a baseball game.
21. The winner in a tournament.

22. A person who makes sure both teams play fair.
23. An action that is against the rules in sports.
27. Something you use to hit a baseball.
29. If you _____ the ball, you throw it to your teammate.
30. A score in which each team has the same number of points.

ACROSS

1. If you **give someone a hard** _____, you cause trouble for that person.

3. If you **miss the** _____, then you didn't understand something.

5. If you **feel under the** _____, you are sick.

7. If you **mend your** _____, then you stop your bad behavior.

10. If your **hands are** _____, then you are unable to help.

11. If something is **a** _____ **for disaster**, it is likely to cause big problems.

12. If something **vanishes into thin** _____, it disappears.

13. If you get **caught** _____ **-handed**, you are discovered committing a crime.

15. If you **face the** _____, you accept criticism or punishment for something you have done.

18. If you **are** _____ **to no good**, you are being bad.

19. If you can **tell two things** _____, you see the differences.

20. If you **rack your** _____, you try hard to remember.

22. If you **give someone the cold** _____, you ignore that person.

24. If you **lend someone a** _____, you help that person.

DOWN

1. If you **throw in the** _____, you give up.

2. If something is **worth your** _____, it is worth your trouble or energy.

3. If you **keep a low** _____, you try not to get noticed.

4. If you stay **through thick and** _____, you are together in good and bad times.

6. If you **keep an** _____ **on something**, you watch it carefully.

8. If you **weather a** _____, you survive a difficult situation.

9. If you **go** _____, you do something excessively.

12. If people **are up in** _____, they are protesting strongly.

14. If something is **just what the** _____ **ordered**, it will solve the problem.

16. If you **are having** _____ **thoughts**, you doubt you made a wise decision.

17. If something is **par for the** _____, it is what you expect it to be.

20. If you **rock the** _____, you cause trouble in a peaceful situation.

21. If something **doesn't** _____ **up**, it doesn't make sense.

23. If you **pull someone's** _____, you are telling a lie to play a joke on that person.

Fixed Phrases

32 Clothing

ACROSS

1. Too small (so that it squeezes you).
3. Article of clothing women may wear instead of a dress.
4. Something you wrap around your neck in winter.
6. A light clothing material used to make T-shirts.
7. Something you wear when you go outside in winter.
9. Something you wear on your feet when you walk outside.
11. Something you wear to keep your hands warm.
15. A shirt for women.
17. Something that holds your pants up.
18. Something you wear on your head.
19. Another word for coat.
20. _____ something on to see if it fits.
21. Another word for used.
23. A very smooth material used to make clothes.
25. Clothes you wear in bed.
26. A pattern with circles: _____ dot.
27. Very popular: A fashion _____.
30. Go well together.
31. A pattern with lines.
32. Something you wear instead of pants in summer.

DOWN

2. A compliment: Those pants look _____ on you!
3. Footwear for the beach.
5. It's the right size: It _____.
8. Too big.
9. An article of clothing that covers your upper body and arms.
10. A material that comes from sheep and is used to make sweaters.
12. What's hot and what's not in clothing.
13. Footwear for hiking.
14. Something you wear over your shirt to keep you warm in winter.
15. Another way to say loose (as in loose pants).
16. Something you wear to keep your feet warm.
17. It's cold: _____ up your coat.
19. Pants made from denim.
22. An article of clothing that women may wear instead of pants.
24. A material that comes from the skin of animals.
25. An article of clothing that covers your legs.
28. Something people wear at a job interview.
29. Something a man wears around his neck when he wears a suit.

🔍 All on a Theme

ACROSS

1. A _____ of lemonade.
3. A _____ of grapes.
6. A _____ of pants.
7. A _____ of bees.
8. A _____ of pancakes.
9. A _____ of whales.
11. A _____ of soup.
12. A _____ of wire.
14. A _____ of garlic.
15. A _____ of chocolates.
17. A _____ of cards.
19. A _____ of kittens.
21. A _____ of cattle.
23. A _____ of sugar.
25. A _____ of leaves.
26. A top ten _____ of things.
27. A _____ of soda pop.
28. A _____ of bread.
29. A _____ of tea.
30. A _____ of lettuce.

DOWN

1. A _____ of jam.
2. A _____ of juice.
3. A _____ of soap.
4. Grab a _____ of peanuts from the bag.
5. A _____ of coffee (on the stove).
6. A _____ of wolves.
8. A _____ of cheese (on your sandwich).
9. A _____ of lions.
10. A _____ of geese.
11. A _____ of potato chips.
13. A _____ of ketchup.
15. A _____ of yarn.
16. A _____ of fish.
17. A _____ of rain.
18. A _____ of ships.
20. A _____ of toothpaste.
22. A _____ of toilet paper.
23. A _____ of potatoes.
24. A _____ of wheat.
25. A _____ of cake.

34 Transportation

2. Transportation that many students take to go to school.

4. Stop! There's a _____ light.

6. Too many cars can cause a traffic _____.

8. Money you pay to ride the bus: Bus _____.

9. A personal form of motorized transportation.

11. Something you should obey while driving: A traffic _____.

13. Transportation with wings.

14. Something that protects your head.

17. A form of transportation that travels on water.

18. Transportation on tracks.

19. A car, truck, or van.

21. A time when many cars are on the road: _____ hour.

22. A small road behind and between buildings.

23. A road where people drive fast.

24. A form of transportation that is used to carry goods.

25. An animal that people ride through the desert.

28. A form of transportation used to send people to space.

31. A person who is walking on the street (not driving a car).

34. An animal that people ride.

35. A place to park: Parking _____.

36. A form of transportation that travels underground.

DOWN

1. A place where pedestrians can cross a road safely.

2. An eco-friendly form of transportation.

3. A road that goes through a neighborhood.

5. A structure that enables a road to go over a river.

7. A person who repairs vehicles.

10. A place where two roads cross.

12. A place where people park their cars (under a roof).

15. A form of transportation meant for one person to ride.

16. A place to drive slowly: A school _____.

20. A form of transportation that many news organizations use to film things from the air.

26. Something drivers wear for safety: A seat _____.

27. A time when you can pass through an intersection: A _____ light.

28. A place where people drive.

29. A place where a road goes through a mountain.

30. How fast you are allowed to drive: The speed _____.

32. A ship that carries people and vehicles from one place to another.

33. Fuel for cars.

🔍 *All on a Theme*

ACROSS

2. Another word for wealthy.
5. A synonym of assault.
8. Another word for pull.
9. Another word for chat.
11. Another word for finish.
13. Another word for error.
16. Another word for close.
17. Another word for correct.
18. Another word for arrive.
19. A synonym of wicked.
20. Another word for summit.
21. A synonym of foe.
24. Another word for ill.
25. A synonym of giggle.
26. Another word for clever.
29. A synonym of hard (to do).
31. Another way to say, "Run fast."
32. Another word for shove.
33. Another word for small.
35. Another word for desire.
36. Another word for mad.

DOWN

1. A synonym of harm.
2. Another word for stone.
3. A synonym of despise.
4. A synonym of recommend.
6. Another word for seat.
7. Another word for weird.
10. A synonym of position.

12. Another way to say, "Talk quietly."
14. A synonym of comprehend.
15. Another word for fortunate.
17. A synonym for recall.
22. A synonym of simple (to do).
23. Another word for shout.

24. Another way to say, "Talk very loudly."
26. Another word for begin.
27. A synonym of reply.
28. Another word for toss.
30. A synonym of rapid.
34. Another word for attempt.

36 Space

ACROSS

2. Space and everything in it.
4. A large object that orbits Earth.
10. Our star.
11. A person who travels to space.
12. The planet we live on.
14. Earth _____ on its axis.
16. A group of stars in the night sky that form a shape.
17. The red planet.
19. A hot glowing ball of gas in space.
20. The planets _____ around the sun.
21. A collection of billions of stars.
23. A ball of ice and dust floating in space.
26. A place where gravity is so strong that not even light can escape: A _____ hole.
27. The hottest planet.
29. The biggest planet.
30. A large object that moves around a star.
31. The shapes of the moon during a month.

DOWN

1. A cloud of gas and dust in space.
3. A vehicle that transports people into space.
5. A planet named after the Roman god of the sea.
6. A rock floating in space.
7. A meteor crashing into Earth: A _____ star.
8. A tool that people use to observe planets.
9. A person who studies space.
13. The name of our galaxy: The _____ Way.
15. A planet famous for its rings.
18. A time when many meteors strike Earth: A meteor _____.
19. The sun and the planets: the _____ system.
21. The force that keeps you on Earth.
22. The path a planet takes around the sun.
23. A hole in the surface of the moon.
24. A time when the moon blocks the sun.
25. A planet that begins with U.
28. Dark places on the sun's surface: Sun _____.

🔍 All on a Theme

ACROSS

3. The season when families go to the beach and kids eat ice cream.

6. The month when children carve jack-o'-lanterns.

7. The time of day when children come home from school.

9. The time of day when the sky starts to lighten (just before sunrise).

12. The season when leaves change color and fall to the ground.

14. A time when very little rain falls and plants begin to wither.

16. A time when farmers gather their crops.

17. A time when roads are busy: _____ hour.

20. A holiday when children wear costumes.

23. A time when the moon blocks the sun.

25. A holiday when children decorate eggs.

26. A holiday when people send cards and chocolates to people they love: _____ Day.

28. The time of day when the sun is at its highest point in the sky.

29. A day when people play tricks on other people: _____ _____ Day. (5,5)

30. The time of day when most people are asleep.

DOWN

1. A time when families take trips.

2. The month when winter begins.

4. The time of day when many people wake up.

5. A time when too much rain causes rivers to overflow and water to cover the ground.

8. A holiday when people make resolutions to change their lives: _____ _____ Day. (3,5)

10. The season when frost covers windows and icicles hang from roofs.

11. The month when people say, "Happy New Year!"

13. The season when animals come out of hibernation and flowers start to bloom.

15. A holiday when Americans eat turkey.

18. A time when things are sold cheaply.

19. A holiday when people hang stockings and give gifts.

21. A time when people vote.

22. A time when people eat cake and get presents.

24. The time of day when many people eat dinner.

27. The time of day when the sky darkens (just after sunset).

38 School Verbs

1. _____ a line at the door.
3. _____ away your books.
6. _____ out how to do something.
9. _____ a documentary.
10. _____ a biography.
11. _____ a math problem.
12. Say how two things are different.
13. _____ your homework.
14. Another way to say comprehend.
18. _____ a snack at recess.
20. Say something in short (including only the important points).
23. Say what something looks like.
24. The opposite of fail.
26. _____ an instrument in music class.
27. _____ a question when you are not sure.
28. _____ a song in music class.
30. Teacher: _____ your books to page 52.

DOWN

2. _____ your hand to ask a question.
3. Guess what will happen.
4. _____ a story.
5. Look at something very carefully.
7. _____ in your homework when it is due.
8. Do poorly on a test.
9. Use a pen and paper.
11. _____ for a test.
12. Say how two things are alike.
13. _____ a picture in art class.
15. _____ a poem to the class.
16. Show how to do something.
17. The opposite of ask.
19. Write down what the teacher says: _____ notes.
21. Teachers _____ your work and give you a grade.
22. Say how to do something.
25. _____ a mistake.
29. _____ on a field trip.

🔍 All on a Theme

ACROSS

4. Giving advice: If I _____ you . . .

5. Greeting: Long _____, no see.

7. Expressing alternative viewpoints: On the other _____ . . .

8. Asking for an opinion: What do you _____?

11. On the phone: Can I _____ you back?

13. Expressing your opinion: In my _____ . . .

15. Ordering: I'd _____ a hamburger, please.

16. At the restaurant: May I take your _____?

17. Giving advice: I think you _____ . . .

18. Summarizing: In _____ . . .

20. Showing agreement: I couldn't have _____ it better myself.

22. Fixed phrase: Better _____ than me.

25. Asking permission: Would you _____ if . . .

27. Showing surprise: You're _____!

28. Rephrasing: What I'm _____ to say is . . .

29. Greeting: How's it _____?

DOWN

1. Rephrasing: To _____ it another way . . .

2. Greeting: How have you _____?

3. Showing surprise: I can't _____ it!

6. Expressing your opinion: If you _____ me . . .

7. Expressing sympathy: I'm sorry to _____ that.

9. At the restaurant: Are you _____ to order?

10. Asking about experience: Have you _____ . . .

12. Saying good-bye: See you _____.

14. Rephrasing: In other _____ . . .

17. Rephrasing: What I'm _____ is . . .

18. On the phone: Can I _____ to Harry please?

19. Saying good-bye: It's been nice _____ to you.

21. Making a suggestion: Why _____ you . . .

23. Fixed phrase: If it were _____ to me . . .

24. Expressing sympathy: That's too _____.

25. Rephrasing: What I _____ is . . .

26. Fixed phrase: As _____ as I'm concerned . . .

Fixed Phrases

ACROSS

2. Regions near the equator: _____ regions.
6. A protected area of water shaped like a horseshoe.
7. Land that is surrounded by water on three sides.
10. The very northern or southern part of the world.
11. Zero degrees latitude.
12. A group of homes and businesses that is smaller than a city but larger than a village.
13. The part of a map that tells you how far apart things on the map are.
15. High, flat land.
16. A place where many people live and work together.
18. A long, flowing body of water.
19. Half of the globe.
20. A place such as Canada, Italy, Japan, or Egypt.
22. A group of mountains: A mountain _____.
24. A body of water completely surrounded by land.
25. A chain of islands.
27. A small group of buildings and homes.
28. A region that receives very little rainfall throughout the year.
29. Lines on a map that are perpendicular to the poles.

DOWN

1. A piece of paper that shows you the location of things.
3. The part of a map that tells you the directions: Compass _____.
4. The regions near the Arctic and Antarctic circles: _____ regions.
5. The height above sea level.
6. The line between two countries.
8. Land that is completely surrounded by water.
9. The opposite of east.
12. Regions between the polar and tropical regions: _____ regions.
13. The opposite of north.
14. Lines on a map that run through the poles.
16. The city where the government of a country is located.
17. Part of a map that tells you what the symbols mean.
20. Large areas of land such as Africa and Australia.
21. A large body of saltwater such as the Atlantic or Pacific.
23. A map of Earth in the shape of a ball.
26. The boundary between land and sea.

All on a Theme

ACROSS

1. Start something happening:
_____ something in motion.

4. End negotiations successfully:
_____ an agreement.

7. Do what someone else does:
_____ someone's lead.

8. Have a party for someone:
_____ a party.

10. Do something important:
_____ a difference.

12. Stop talking about something:
_____ the subject.

14. Start sobbing uncontrollably:
_____ into tears.

16. Tell somebody something the
person didn't know: _____
the news.

17. Smile for the camera:
_____ cheese.

18. Say what you are thinking:
_____ your mind.

20. Be polite: _____ your
manners.

21. Use a pencil to create art:
_____ a picture.

22. Give someone the salt while at
the table: _____ the salt.

24. Tell stories about someone:
_____ gossip.

DOWN

2. Say something threatening:
_____ tough.

3. Talk about something when
you know nothing about it:
_____ your mouth off.

5. Break the law: _____ a
crime.

6. Put a jacket on a chair for a
friend: _____ a seat. Hint:
It begins with S.

7. Learn something: _____
out something.

9. Win a lot of money: _____
the jackpot.

11. Receive a tip: _____ the
change.

13. Advertise: _____ an ad in
a newspaper.

14. Bribe someone: _____
somebody off.

15. Prevent someone from doing
something: _____ in
someone's way.

17. Run away without telling
anyone: _____ town.

19. Do something dangerous:
_____ with fire.

20. Lose an opportunity:
_____ your chance.

21. Serve a jail sentence:
_____ time.

23. Stir up trouble: _____
problems.

25. Indicate you want to ask a
question: _____ your
hand.

42 Fitness and Health

4. A type of exercise used to strengthen stomach muscles: _____-ups.

6. Health advice: _____ smoking.

9. A place where people work out.

10. How long you can keep doing an activity.

12. A type of nutrition you can get from meat.

14. Exercise: _____ out.

16. An activity you do on a mountain trail.

22. A type of exercise done with a rope.

23. Not healthy: _____ of shape.

24. Health advice: Cut _____ on junk food.

27. Calcium, sodium, and potassium.

29. People on a diet often count the _____ they eat.

30. A good mix of healthy food: A _____ diet.

32. Step on a _____ to check your weight.

33. See a doctor once a year: Have a _____up.

DOWN

1. _____ weights to gain strength.

2. A relaxing exercise that involves lots of stretching.

3. A type of exercise: _____ jacks.

5. Someone who helps you plan your exercise.

7. An activity you do in a pool.

8. A health concern: High _____ pressure.

11. Fast-paced exercise that is usually done to music.

13. A type of exercise to strengthen your arms and shoulders: _____-ups.

15. Try to get healthy: Get in _____ .

17. An activity you can do in the park.

18. Racket sports and video games can improve your hand-eye _____ .

19. Another word for stamina.

20. Something you use to dry yourself off.

21. You should _____ your muscles before you do hard exercise.

25. A person who plays a sport.

26. How fast you pump blood: Your _____ rate.

27. Tissue that helps your body move.

28. How fast you do something.

30. Hard tissue that helps supports your body.

31. One way to lose weight: Go on a _____ .

🔍 All on a Theme

ACROSS

2. A large group of people that rhymes with loud.

3. A Halloween costume that rhymes with rich.

4. A piece of furniture that rhymes with cable.

5. A type of weather that rhymes with dog.

8. A utensil that rhymes with pork.

10. A high playing card that rhymes with black.

12. A crop that rhymes with mice.

13. A number that rhymes with pen.

14. A number that rhymes with wait.

17. A part of a bear that rhymes with saw.

19. A fruit that rhymes with hair.

21. A direction that rhymes with mouth.

23. A color that rhymes with do.

24. A forest animal that rhymes with here.

25. A direction that rhymes with least.

27. A type of weather that rhymes with plane.

28. A color that rhymes with hello.

30. A month that rhymes with hay.

32. A large sea that rhymes with potion.

35. A small river that rhymes with dream.

DOWN

1. A body part that rhymes with fed.

2. A piece of furniture that rhymes with care.

3. A direction that rhymes with best.

6. A color that rhymes with bean.

7. A crop that rhymes with born.

8. A body part that rhymes with put.

9. A toy on a string that rhymes with sight.

10. A month that rhymes with tune.

11. A utensil that rhymes with life.

15. A farm animal that rhymes with source.

16. An instrument that rhymes with toot.

18. A crop that rhymes with beat.

19. A fruit that rhymes with thumb.

20. A fruit that rhymes with merry.

22. A part of a turtle that rhymes with tell.

23. A forest animal that rhymes with hair.

24. A musical instrument that rhymes with crumb.

26. A utensil that rhymes with moon.

29. A group of animals that rhymes with word.

31. A body part that rhymes with farm.

33. A farm animal that rhymes with how.

34. A high playing card that rhymes with base.

Word Skills 📝

44 Fantasy

3. A horse with a horn.

6. An evil spell.

8. A person who does great deeds.

10. Genie: I will _____ you three wishes.

11. A robber who attacks people traveling in the mountains and forests.

13. A mischievous little green monster.

14. Something a genie makes comes true.

15. An old story (often about a hero).

19. A little magical winged creature.

20. Something you need to find buried treasure: A treasure _____.

21. A very large person.

22. A woman who can use magic.

24. Can't be seen.

27. Another word for wizard.

29. A large fire-breathing reptile.

31. A person that can change into a wolf.

33. Something witches cast.

34. A woman who turns people to stone in Greek myths.

35. A monster that is sometimes found under bridges.

DOWN

1. A person who attacks ships to steal their treasure.

2. A set of human bones.

4. A hole in a mountain.

5. A man who can use magic.

7. A walking corpse.

8. A _____ house has a ghost inside it.

9. A person who wears armor and rides a horse.

12. A short person (known for mining jewels).

15. A place where some genies live.

16. A monster that drinks people's blood.

17. An old story that explains something.

18. If you put someone _____ your spell, you control that person through magic.

23. A place where knights live.

25. If you _____ the spell, you stop the spell from working.

26. A large cruel monster that eats humans. Hint: It begins with O.

28. A giant with one eye in Greek myths.

29. A very dry place.

30. A wizard can _____ a spell.

32. A stick with magic powers.

🔍 *All on a Theme*

ACROSS

2. Something people send in the mail.
5. Something people drive.
7. Something people read.
8. Things that people wash after dinner.
9. A thing that kids use to catch butterflies and dragonflies.
11. A thing that people wink.
12. Something people shrug.
14. Something people sleep on.
15. A thing that people wear on their heads.
17. Something people watch at the theater.
19. Something you comb.
20. A thing that birds build.
24. Something you make at the beach.
27. A thing that spiders make to catch flies.
29. An animal that people ride.
30. A thing that birds lay.
32. Something people watch at home.
33. A thing that people fly.
34. Something you catch with a hook.
35. Something people stomp when they are angry.

DOWN

1. Something you open when it's hot inside your house or apartment.
3. A thing that you answer when it rings.
4. Something people slam.
5. Something you eat on your birthday.
6. Something people play.
7. A thing that people bounce.
9. Something people blow when they are sick.
10. Things that you brush before going to bed.
13. A thing you open when it rains.
16. A thing that people study for.
17. Something people spend.
18. Something you turn on when it's dark.
21. A device that people listen to.
22. A thing that people wear to protect their head.
23. Something you grow in your garden. Hint: It begins with F.
24. A thing that you make when it snows.
25. A utensil that people eat soup with.
26. Something you sit on.
28. An insect that stings.
31. A thing that people give.

46 Feelings

ACROSS

2. Really wanting to know something.
5. Another word for envious.
8. How you would feel if you worked hard all day.
11. If you think that things will be bad in the future, you feel _____ .
12. How you would feel if your child were very sick and in the hospital.
13. The feeling of wanting what other people have.
14. How you would feel if you were going to do something that you really wanted to do.
16. Another word for scared.
17. How you would feel if you wanted a drink.
19. If you pour your _____ out, you express your feelings.
21. Another word for afraid.
23. How you would feel if you hadn't eaten all day.
25. How you would feel if you found out you were walking around with your zipper undone.
27. How you would feel if you walked around without a coat on in winter.
28. Another way to say unhappy or sad.

DOWN

1. If you _____ in love with someone, you begin to love that person.
2. If you don't understand something, you feel _____ .
3. If you think things will be good in the future, you feel _____ .
4. Another word for angry.
6. How you would feel if something happened that you didn't expect.
7. Another word for worried.
9. If you feel that you can do anything you want, you feel _____ .
10. How you would feel if your vacation got canceled.
15. Another word for cold.
18. How you would feel if somebody broke your things on purpose.
19. How you would feel if you wore a sweater in summer.
20. How you would feel if someone kept bugging you. Hint: It begins with A.
21. Excited because you are going to do something: Looking _____ to doing something.
22. If you _____ your feelings, you say how you feel.
24. How you would feel if your child won first place in a contest.
26. How you would feel if your best friend moved away.

46

🔍 All on a Theme

ACROSS

1. What time does your alarm _____ **off**?
2. You have to _____ **up to** your problems.
4. Do you recycle cans? Or do you just _____ them **away**?
6. Because of the recession, the company had to _____ **off** workers.
7. Did you _____ **in on** the meeting?
8. I won't _____ **up with** the noise any longer!
9. You can _____ it **off** our list.
11. I've been away so I want to _____ **up on** the news.
13. If you _____ **up to** someone, you respect that person.
14. It was a great day to _____ **out on** a new journey.
15. You have to _____ **out of** the hotel before 11 o'clock.
17. Slow down or you'll _____ **up** in the hospital!
19. If you _____ **out of** something, you use it all up.
20. _____ **out of** your account when you are finished.
21. If you _____ something **over**, you redo it.
22. If you _____ someone **off**, you scold that person.
23. If you _____ someone **off**, you cheat that person.

DOWN

1. Let's _____ **together** at 4 o'clock.
2. I won't _____ **for** that old trick.
3. They really _____ it **off** from the first time they met.
5. _____ **out**! You nearly hit me.
7. Could you _____ **by** the bakery and pick up some bread?
8. Can you _____ **up** the pencils that I dropped on the floor?
10. Did you _____ **to** your diet?
12 My doctor told me to _____ **down on** meat.
13. If you _____ **through** something, you survive a terrible experience.
14. He wears really bright clothes that make him _____ **out** in a crowd.
16. If you _____ **off** an event, that means you cancel it.
18. I'll _____ **by** his house and pay him a visit.

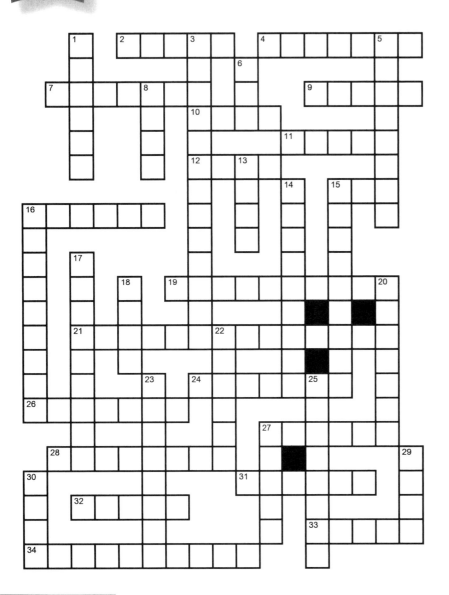

2. Liquid rock inside the Earth.
4. A scientific way to say "pull together."
7. Another way to say "bend light."
9. Energy you can hear.
10. A form of energy that makes things hot.
11. How an animal is born, lives, reproduces, and dies: A life _____ .
12. How much matter something has.
15. A state of matter that expands to fill its container (like oxygen).
16. Anything that has mass and occupies space.
19. An instrument that is used to see tiny objects like cells.
21. A person who studies extinct animals.
24. Another way to say "bounce light."
26. See how big, wide, hot, or heavy something is.
27. A large object that orbits a star.
28. How fast something is moving.
31. The remains of an animals or plant from long ago.
32. The state of matter that maintains its shape (like wood or a rock).
33. A push or a pull (like gravity or friction).
34. A person who studies space.

DOWN

1. Change from liquid to solid.
3. A person who solves equations.
5. Change from gas to a liquid.
6. Your genetic code.
8. An imaginary line that something turns on.
13. A hot, glowing ball of gas in space.
14. A tool used to observe things in space.

15. A person who studies rocks.
16. The force that attracts some metal objects like iron.
17. Change from liquid to gas.
18. Change from solid to liquid.
20. A scientific way to say "that an animal no longer exists."
22. In science, an explanation for why something happens.

23. The force that slows down moving things that are touching.
25. A scientific way to say "separate into groups."
27. Show that a theory is correct.
29. The end of a magnet.
30. Information that you gather.

All on a Theme

ACROSS

3. Musicians _____ musical instruments.
4. Chefs _____ food.
6. Movie stars _____ in movies.
7. Bakers _____ bread.
8. Hairdressers _____ hair.
12. Janitors _____ buildings.
13. Scientists _____ experiments.
14. Police officers _____ crimes.
15. Architects _____ buildings.
17. Authors _____ articles and stories.
18. Farmers _____ crops.
19. Photographers _____ pictures.
20. Waiters _____ food.
21. Ranchers _____ cattle.
23. Doctors _____ sick people.

DOWN

1. Pilots _____ airplanes.
2. Travel agents _____ airline tickets and hotels for you.
3. Firefighters _____ out fires.
5. Police officers _____ criminals.
7. Construction workers _____ houses.
9. Comedians _____ jokes.
10. Factory workers _____ things.
11. Singers _____ songs.
13. Mail carriers _____ mail.
14. Tailors _____ clothes.
15. Truck drivers _____ trucks.
16. Mechanics _____ cars.
18. Cashiers _____ you your change.
19. Teachers _____ children.
20. Salespeople _____ things.
22. Artists _____ pictures.

50 The Human Body

1. Tissue that helps you move.
7. Breathe out.
8. A tissue that connects muscles to bones.
9. Organs that you use to breathe.
11. A tissue that connects bones to bones.
12. Body parts you walk on.
14. Break down food inside your body.
16. Hard parts inside your mouth that you use to chew.
17. The organ system that controls your body.
20. The organ system that moves blood around your body.
24. A joint in the middle of your arm.
26. An organ that lets you think.
28. A joint in the middle of your leg.
30. A part of your body you use to grab things.
31. A joint that connects your hand and arm.

DOWN

2. A hard, flexible tissue found in your ear and nose.
3. Breathe in.
4. Body parts you use to touch things and to point.
5. An organ that pumps blood.
6. The organ system that breaks down food.
10. The organ system that gives your body support.
12. Tissue that is used to store energy and keep you warm.

13. Parts of your foot that have nails.
15. An organ that digests food.
16. An organ you use to taste things, talk, and move food around your mouth.
17. Tissue that sends signals throughout your body.
18. The organ system that takes in oxygen and releases carbon dioxide.
19. A body part you use to smell.
21. Bones that protect your lungs.

22. A joint that connects your leg and foot.
23. The lower part of your mouth.
25. A red liquid that carries oxygen and nutrients around the body.
26. A hard structure in your body that supports you and gives you shape.
27. The part of your body that holds your head up.
29. The parts of your body you use to see.

All on a Theme

ACROSS

2. The opposite of lose (as in lose your wallet).
3. The antonym of lend (as in lend some money).
6. The opposite of send (as in send a message).
9. The opposite of open (as in open a window).
10. The opposite of love.
11. The antonym of freeze.
12. The antonym of start.
14. The antonym of throw.
16. The opposite of win.
17. The antonym of empty (as in empty a bucket).
19. The opposite of confess.
20. The antonym of break.
21. The antonym of separate. Hint: It begins with C.
22. The opposite of sit (as in sit down).
24. The antonym of expand.
26. The opposite of work.
28. The antonym of enter (as in enter a building).
29. The antonym of permit (as in permit someone to do something).
30. The opposite of live.

DOWN

1. The antonym of defend.
2. The opposite of lead (as in lead someone somewhere).
3. The opposite of doubt (as in doubt what somebody says).
4. The opposite of walk.
5. The opposite of shout.
6. The antonym of forget.
7. The opposite of compliment (as in compliment someone for doing something well).
8. The opposite of hit (as in hit the bull's-eye).
13. The opposite of push.
15. The antonym of laugh.
18. The antonym of put down (as in put down your pencil). (4,2)
19. The antonym of create.
20. The opposite of pass (as in pass an exam).
23. The opposite of depart.
24. The antonym of save.
25. The antonym of lower (as in lower the bridge).
26. The opposite of take off (as in take off your coat). (3,2)
27. The antonym of ask.

52 Crime and Punishment

1. The crime of breaking public property.
7. A place where trials are held.
8. Steal from a store.
9. Bring goods into a country illegally.
10. A person who saw someone commit a crime.
13. Money paid as punishment for breaking the law.
16. A rule made by the government.
17. Things that prove somebody committed a crime.
21. Commit a crime: _____ the law.
22. The crime of killing someone.
23. A person who has suffered a crime.
25. A person who steals your wallet on the street or subway.
27. A high-ranking police officer who solves serious crimes.
28. In jail: Behind _____.
29. Evidence taken from blood or saliva.
31. The opposite of guilty.
32. A person who presides over a court.

DOWN

2. Say somebody committed a crime.
3. A person who the police think may have done a crime.
4. The process of determining if a person is innocent or guilty.
5. Interview a suspect.
6. A person who catches criminals. (6,7)
11. The punishment a judge hands down.

12. The crime of threatening to reveal a secret unless someone gives you money.
14. A story that proves your innocence.
15. Go to jail for a while: Do _____.
18. Found guilty of a crime in a court of law.
19. Catch and hold someone because he or she is suspected of committing a crime.

20. A group of people who decide whether a person is guilty or innocent.
24. Be officially accused of a crime: Be _____ with a crime.
26. A place where criminals are kept.
30. Not get punished for committing a crime: Get _____ with a crime.

🔍 All on a Theme

ACROSS

1. The city where you can find the Statue of Liberty. (3,4)
6. The city that was home to Greek democracy in ancient times.
7. A country where many Aztec ruins are located.
9. The country where Hinduism and Buddhism originated.
11. The country where Islam originated. (5,6)
12. The continent where the Rocky Mountains are found. (5,7)
16. The city where the Eiffel Tower is located.
19. The country that is known for koalas and kangaroos.
22. The ocean that is located between Europe and the Americas.
24. The country that is home to the Pyramids.
26. The continent through which the Nile River flows.
27. The city where the 1936 Olympics were held. Hint: The first letter is B.
28. The city to which many Muslim people make a pilgrimage.

Places Around the World

DOWN

2. The country where Moscow is located.
3. The country in which the Great Wall is located.
4. The ocean where the Hawaiian Islands are located.
5. A large city that is located on the Thames River.
8. The ocean that surrounds the North Pole.

10. The continent where Italy and Denmark are located.
13. The continent that is home to emperor penguins.
14. The ocean located between Australia and Africa.
15. The continent where Korea and Thailand are located.
17. The continent on which the Andes Mountains are located. (5,7)

18. A country through which the Amazon River flows.
20. The country in which Madrid is located.
21. The country where Mt. Fuji is located.
23. The country where the Olympics originated.
25. A country where many Inca ruins are located.

1. A green form of transportation.
5. Conserve water by spending less time in the _____.
7. An _____ animal is an animal that belongs to a species that does not exist anymore.
8. Conserve energy by turning off _____ when you are not using them.
9. Harmful substances: _____ chemicals.
10. Anything that makes nature dirty.
14. Power that comes from the sun.
16. Cups you use then throw away: _____ cups.
18. Harmful rain caused by pollution: _____ rain.
19. Conserve natural resources when you _____ bottles, cans, and paper.
22. Use an object again.
23. Eco-_____ products are products that don't harm the environment.
24. Food that is grown without pesticides or chemical fertilizers.
26. Global warming: _____ change.
28. Conserve energy by wearing a _____ inside instead of using heat.
29. April 22nd: _____ Day.
30. Raising the Earth's temperature due to gases that trap heat: The _____ effect.

DOWN

2. Throw garbage on the ground.
3. Conserve water by turning off faucets while _____ your teeth.
4. The rise in the Earth's average temperature: Global _____.
6. A chemical that is used to kill unwanted plants and animals.
11. A large area where garbage is buried.
12. Things we throw away.
13. Destruction of wildlife homes: Habitat _____.
15. Conserve water by fixing a _____ faucet.
17. A layer in the atmosphere that protects the Earth from UV light: _____ layer.
20. A greenhouse gas: _____ dioxide.
21. An _____ animal is an animal that belongs to a species with very few members left.
22. Use less of something.
25. Another way to say eco-friendly.
27. Another word for garbage.

🔍 All on a Theme

ACROSS

1. Sign on a property: No _____. Hint: It begins with T.
4. Salesclerk: Did you _____ what you were looking for?
5. Sign in a restaurant: Please wait to be _____.
7. Waiter: Would you like _____ to drink with that?
8. Sign in a store: No refunds without a valid _____.
12. Cashier in a fast food restaurant: Is that for _____ or to go?
13. Train conductor: May I see your _____ please?
16. Sign above a door.
17. Flight attendant: Please fasten your _____ _____. (4,5)
19. Customer at a bank: I'd like to _____ this money into my account.
21. Cashier: With _____ that comes to $31.56.
22. Doctor: Get some _____.
23. Sign at a business: _____ wanted.
25. Teacher: _____ your books to page 45.
27. Sign in a zoo: Don't _____ the animals.
28. Doctor: Drink plenty of _____.
29. Doctor: Where does it _____?
30. Sign by a road: _____ when wet.

DOWN

2. Waiter: Are you _____ to order?
3. Sign in a store: _____ will be prosecuted.
4. Sign by a lake: No _____.
5. Customer at the theater: I'd like two tickets for the 8:00 _____.
6. Salesclerk: Are you looking for anything in _____.
9. Customer at a gas station: Can you _____ the oil?
10. Teacher: Your homework is _____ next Monday.
11. Sign in front of a fire extinguisher: In _____ of emergency.
14. Teacher: _____ out your social studies textbooks please.
15. Police officer: May I see your driver's _____?
18. Cashier: Your _____ comes to $17.56.
20. Pilot: We are preparing for _____. (4-3)
24. Customer at a theater: I'd like a large _____ and two colas.
25. Waiter: May I take your _____?
26. Customer at a gas station: _____ it up please.

1. Another way to say right (as in the answer was right).

3. A form of transportation that many students take to school.

5. A group of students who study together.

7. A subject where you multiply and divide numbers.

8. When you hand in homework: The _____ date.

9. The study of the past.

10. _____ a test to show how much you have learned.

14. A person who studies.

16. The head of a school.

17. Write down what your teacher says: Take _____.

19. Read so everyone can hear you: Read _____ loud.

20. Where students do work.

22. Something teachers write on with chalk.

24. A subject where you draw.

25. _____ a question when you are not sure.

26. A picture that shows the relationship between two things (such as population over time).

31. A subject where you play instruments.

33. A subject where you learn about solids, liquids, and gases.

34. _____ a math problem.

35. _____ your hand when you want to ask a question.

DOWN

2. A person who teaches.

3. A student who threatens other students.

4. Another way to say comprehend.

6. The study of people and places: _____ studies.

7. See how big, long, or heavy something is.

11. Something that shows you the locations of things.

12. Do something wrong: Make a _____.

13. Something you use to cut paper.

15. A book you use in class.

16. Something you write with.

18. Teachers _____ your homework and give it back to you.

21. Something you use to correct mistakes.

23. Work that the teachers tells you to do.

27. The _____ to the question is at the back of the book.

28. Why something happens: _____ and effect.

29. Another word for student.

30. Go somewhere with your class: Go on a _____ trip.

32. The opposite of fail.

🔍 *All on a Theme*

ACROSS

1. Play basketball: _____ some hoops.
3. Not succeed: _____ in your attempt.
5. Start a business: _____ into business.
6. Gossip: _____ behind someone's back.
7. Be an example for others: _____ the standard.
8. Receive a tip: _____ the change.
10. Not be able to remember: _____ a blank.
12. Delay something to give yourself more time: _____ time.
13. Make somebody look foolish: _____ a trick on somebody.
14. Make a law (as in a government vote): _____ a law.
16. Use a camera: _____ a picture.
17. Stop something sinister: _____ the world.
18. Tell stories about someone: _____ gossip.
21. Steal: _____ a crime.
23. Advertise: _____ an ad in a magazine.
24. Use soap: _____ your hands.
26. Destroy something: _____ damage.
27. Have a problem with your eyesight: _____ double.

DOWN

1. Be noticeable: _____ out.
2. Say something that isn't true: _____ a lie.
3. Deal with a difficult situation: _____ a problem.
4. Think you are better than someone: _____ down on a person.
5. Quit: _____ up.
7. Talk to God: _____ a prayer.
9. Say something nice: _____ someone a compliment.
11. Spend your money foolishly: _____ your money.
12. Start laughing loudly: _____ into laughter.
13. Publish: _____ something in print.
15. Understand what somebody is saying: _____ someone's drift.
17. Miss a meal: _____ lunch.
19. Decide when you will do something: _____ a date. Hint: It begins with F.
20. Manage to contact someone on the phone: _____ a person.
22. Arrive at the station late: _____ the train.
25. Say what you are thinking: _____ your mind.

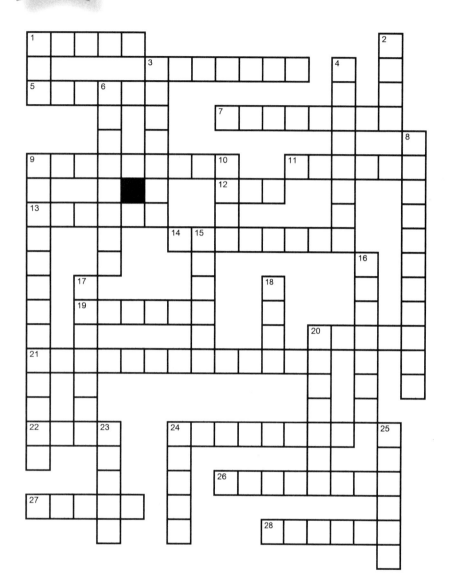

1. Something that is measured in degrees.
3. The "point" in 4.62.
5. Calculate the quotient of two numbers.
7. A shape with three sides.
9. The distance around a shape.
11. An angle that is greater than 90 degrees.
12. 1, 3, 5, 7, 9, 11: _____ numbers.
13. The distance from the center of a circle to the edge.
14. Guess how much something is approximately.
19. The _____ of a cube is length times width times height.
20. A location in space represented by a dot.
21. The distance around a circle.
22. The _____ of a square is length times width.
24. _____ lines never cross.
26. Two-thirds, one-half, or three-sevenths.
27. How wide something is.
28. How high something is.

DOWN

1. Calculate the sum of two numbers.
2. A box with six equal sides.
3. What angles are measured in.
4. Numbers less than zero: _____ numbers.
6. Without limit.
8. The bottom part of a fraction.

9. _____ lines cross each other at right angles.
10. Three is the square _____ of nine.
15. The shape of a ball.
16. Another way to say highest. Hint: It begins with M.
17. The _____ of A and B: (A+B)/2.

18. 2, 4, 6, 8, 10, 12: _____ numbers.
20. The number of parts per 100.
23. An angle that is less than 90 degrees.
24. 2, 3, 5, 7, 11: _____ numbers.
25. How long something is.

All on a Theme

ACROSS

1. The past participle of rise.
3. The past participle of bite.
5. The past participle of bring.
8. The past participle of ring.
11. The past participle of drive.
13. The past participle of eat.
14. The past participle of swim.
16. The past participle of shine.
17. The past participle of burn.
18. The past participle of feel.
19. The past participle of choose.
21. The past participle of strike.
22. The past participle of grow.
24. The past participle of speak.
25. The past participle of forbid.
27. The past participle of tell.
29. The past participle of blow.
30. The past participle of know.
31. The past participle of sing.
32. The past participle of wear.

DOWN

2. The past participle of see.
4. The past participle of tear.
6. The past participle of go.
7. The past participle of throw.
8. The past participle of ride.
9. The past participle of give.
10. The past participle of do.
12. The past participle of be.
15. The past participle of mistake.
16. The past participle of sting.
18. The past participle of forget.
20. The past participle of find.
23. The past participle of shrink.
24. The past participle of sink.
25. The past participle of fly.
26. The past participle of drink.
28. The past participle of draw.

ACROSS

4. Another word for dirt.
7. The parts of a tree that change color during the fall.
9. A large body of saltwater.
10. A small, rounded mountain.
11. Water form that rises and falls as it travels.
12. A hole in a mountain.
13. A very dry biome that gets very little rainfall throughout the year.
14. Something that comes in and out at the beach.
15. Water that forms on leaves during cool nights.
20. A frozen, treeless land in the far north.
21. A high, flat area of land.
22. A large chunk of ice that floats in the ocean.
23. Celestial bodies that shine at night.
24. A forest that gets lots of precipitation.
27. A celestial body that reflects sunlight and goes through phases.
29. A biome found high in the mountains. Hint: It begins with A.
31. A small river.
32. A grassy biome with some trees in Africa.
33. In the sky, something bright and colorful that forms after it rains.
34. Land between two mountains.

DOWN

1. Frozen water that forms on windows during winter.
2. A celestial body that shines during the day.
3. A body of freshwater that is surrounded by land.
5. Flashes of light during a storm.
6. A sandy shore next to the ocean.
8. A dark area formed by blocking sunlight.

11. A wet biome where ducks and frogs live.
16. A large, high, rocky landform.
17. A large body of ice that does not melt away during the summer.
18. A grassy biome where bison live.
19. Water that flows over a cliff.
22. Ice that hangs from your roof.

23. The land next to a body of water.
25. A raised area of land or coral just under the surface of the water.
26. A piece of snow.
28. A mountain that erupts from time to time.
30. The top of a mountain.

All on a Theme

ACROSS

1. Articles of clothing you wear on your hands.
5. A part of your body that you use to touch.
6. A piece of furniture that people sleep on.
7. A part of your body that you use to hear.
8. An article of clothing that you wear instead of pants.
9. Parts of a bicycle you push down on to make the bicycle move.
10. A part of a plant that gathers water.
12. A part of a ship that is used to steer it.
15. A part of your body that you use to smell.
17. A part of a web page that you view.
18. A part of a ship where people walk.
20. A part of a boat that catches wind.
21. A part of a web page that you read.
23. A part of a plant that uses sunlight to make food.
26. A part of a web page that you click.
27. A piece of jewelry that you wear around your neck.
30. A piece of furniture that many people can sit on.
31. A part of a bicycle that you use to steer.

DOWN

1. A branch of mathematics that deals with shapes and angles.
2. A branch of the military that protects a country's skies.
3. A part of your body that pumps blood.
4. A part of a plant that blooms.
6. A piece of jewelry that you wear on your wrist.
8. A part of a plant that can make new plants.
11. A part of a tree that holds the tree up.

13. A part of your body that you use to see.
14. Parts of a fish that let it breathe underwater.
16. A part of a plant that holds the plant up.
19. A part of a bicycle that connects the pedals to the back wheel.
20. A part of your body that you use to digest food.
22. A part of a fish that it uses to move.

23. A part of your body that you use to breathe.
24. A branch of mathematics that deals with solving for *x* and *y*.
25. A piece of furniture that people eat off of.
28. A piece of furniture that one person can sit on.
29. A branch of the military that protects a country's land.
30. Articles of clothing that keep your feet warm.

1. An event in which athletes jump over a bar: _____ jump.
5. An event in which teams hit a ball over a net using their hands.
7. An event in which athletes jump off a board into a pool.
10. A person who participates in sports.
12. The summer Olympics are held every _____ years.
13. An event in which athletes balance and tumble.
18. The country someone is from.
20. Something given to the top three athletes.
21. An event in which athletes fight with a very thin sword.
23. The medal that goes to second place.
24. An event in which athletes jump as far as they can: _____ jump.
27. The best time or score.
28. A person who makes sure teams play fair.
29. The medal that goes to third place.

2. The medal that goes to first place.
3. A person who decides the winner in sports like diving and gymnastics.
4. An event in which athletes ride bicycles.
6. The song of a country.
8. An event in which athletes use a pole to jump over a very high bar: Pole _____.
9. An event in which athletes shoot a bow and arrow.

11. Something that is carried before the Olympics begin.
14. An event in which athletes throw a very heavy ball: _____ put.
15. An event that takes place in a pool.
16. The symbol of the Olympics: Five _____.
17. A race in which athletes jump over obstacles.

19. Events that include running, jumping, and throwing: _____ and field.
20. A very long run.
22. A person who blocks or stops shots in some team sports.
24. Once around the track.
25. A place where the medalists stand.
26. A short, fast run.
27. A team race in which athletes pass a baton: A _____ race.

All on a Theme

ACROSS

2. Don't count your _____ before they hatch.

8. Look before you _____.

10. Rome wasn't built in a _____.

11. You _____ what you sow.

12. You can lead a _____ to water, but you can't make it drink.

15. Misery loves _____.

17. Let sleeping _____ lie.

18. Great minds think _____.

20. Walls have _____.

22. Seeing is _____.

23. Money is the root of all _____.

24. Out of _____, out of mind.

26. _____ makes waste.

28. Easy come, easy _____.

30. A poor workman always blames his _____.

32. When it _____, it pours.

33. No news is _____ news.

34. Practice what you _____.

35. Fight fire with _____.

36. _____ before pleasure.

37. The _____ cannot change its spots.

DOWN

1. That which does not _____ us makes us stronger.

3. Talk is _____.

4. The _____ justifies the means.

5. Give a man a _____ and you feed him for a day.

6. There's _____ in numbers.

7. To _____ is human.

9. _____ makes perfect.

13. You can't teach an old _____ new tricks.

14. Don't rock the _____.

16. _____ is better than cure.

17. Better the _____ you know.

19. There's no such thing as a free _____.

21. Every cloud has a _____ lining.

22. _____ can't be choosers.

24. Better _____ than sorry.

25. Don't put all your _____ in one basket.

27. _____ speaks louder than words.

29. _____ makes right.

31. If at first you don't _____, try, try again.

34. No _____, no gain.

Fixed Phrases

1. Spend time with someone: _____ out together.
4. A sibling who was born at the same time as you.
8. Somebody you know but not well enough to consider as a friend.
9. Invite someone to go on a date with you: _____ someone out.
14. Have similar interests: Have a lot in _____.
15. An uncle, aunt, or cousin.
16. If you _____ in touch with someone, that means you contact that person occasionally.
18. Always have a good time together: Get _____ well with someone.
21. The woman in a married couple.
22. Date a person: Go _____ with someone.
23. Without a boyfriend or girlfriend; without a wife or husband.
24. The person who tells you what to do at work.
25. A friend you can tell your problems to: A _____ friend.
28. A person who lives near you.
30. A man who is about to get married.
31. Some people _____ their friends instead of calling them.
32. A person who teaches and inspires you.

DOWN

1. The man in a married couple.
2. A reason to break up: Irreconcilable _____.
3. A person who helps you learn.
5. Stop dating a person: _____ up with someone.
6. Ideal partner: Has a _____ of humor.
7. A ring that means you are going to get married: An _____ ring.
10. Dating a person regularly: _____ someone.
11. Lose interest in a person: Grow _____.
12. A woman who is about to get married.
13. A person you work with.
17. Ask someone to marry you.
19. Fight with words.
20. Another way to say brother or sister.
21. A ceremony in which people get married.
26. Love at first _____.
27. Ideal partner: _____ -looking.
29. Get along really well right from the first time you meet: _____ it off with someone.

🔍 All on a Theme

ACROSS

1. Meat that is easy to cut and chew: _____ meat.
4. Go down quickly: A _____ decline.
7. Fruit that has been picked recently: _____ fruit.
9. A teacher who has many rules and punishments: A _____ teacher.
12. A time of prosperity or cultural achievement: A _____ age.
15. Something bad that has to be done: A _____ evil.
18. A small problem: A _____ setback.
19. A price that is not at all expensive: A _____ price.
22. A bribe: _____ money.
24. The noise around you: _____ noise.
25. A wise suggestion: A _____ idea.
26. A trial that is impartial: A _____ trial.

DOWN

2. Only mom, dad, and children living together: A _____ family.
3. Money you didn't have to work hard for: _____ money.
5. Very old furniture: _____ furniture.
6. Immediate payment: _____ payment.
8. A parent raising children without the help of a spouse: A _____ parent.

10. A trip without any troubles: A _____ journey.
11. A friend that you know very well: A _____ friend.
13. Someone you don't know very well: A _____ acquaintance.
14. A huge effect: A _____ impact.
16. Criticism that helps you improve: _____ criticism.
17. Many cars on the road: _____ traffic.

18. A sauce that isn't spicy: A _____ sauce.
20. History of very long ago: _____ history.
21. A healthy, full meal: A _____ meal.
22. Lots of money to spend: _____ pockets.
23. A daily workout: _____ exercise.
26. Hot dogs, hamburgers, or pizza: _____ food.

ACROSS

2. End your job when you are old.

4. A document that summarizes your education, skills, and work experience.

7. Stop working: _____ your job.

10. Getting skills or knowledge.

12. A person who works for a company.

14. Lose your job: Get _____.

15. A job where you only work two or three days a week: _____-time.

17. Pay somebody to work for you.

18. A legal agreement between an employee and employer.

20. A time when employers ask job applicants questions.

21. A time when the roads are busy because many people are driving to or from work: _____ hour.

22. The amount of money that the government takes from your salary: _____ tax.

24. Travel to and from work.

26. Things you can do.

27. Work at night: Do the night _____. Hint: It begins with SH.

28. A time when workers refuse to work until their demands are met.

29. Extra money that employers give employees.

DOWN

1. A document you fill out when you apply for a job: An application _____.

2. Tell your boss that you quit your job.

3. Least amount of money employers can pay: _____ wage.

5. Ask to work at a company: _____ for a job.

6. Your salary after taxes are deducted.

7. Things you need to get a job.

8. A job where you work eight hours a day, five days a week: _____-time.

9. Things you get from a job on top of your salary. Hint: It begins with B.

11. Something employers offer employees to make them work harder.

12. A company that hires someone.

13. If you have worked before, you have work _____.

16. The amount of money an employee earns in an hour.

17. We need workers: _____ wanted.

19. A person who tells you what to do at your workplace.

23. The amount of money an employee earns every month or every year.

25. A group of workers who get together to protect worker rights.

🔍 All on a Theme

ACROSS

1. A Halloween greeting: _____-or-treat!

4. The whole day: From _____ to dusk.

6. A path for trains.

8. A dirty hit: _____ the belt.

10. A place for cowboys: The _____ West.

12. Assist someone: Lend a _____ hand.

14. A friendly greeting: A _____ welcome.

15. Revenge: _____ for tat.

16. Find ways to save money: _____ corners.

18. Have more important things to do: Have bigger _____ to fry.

19. Carbon dioxide: A _____ gas.

21. Nice to look at: _____ as a picture.

22. Be careful: _____ before you leap!

23. A person who worries too much.

26. Wait! _____ your horses!

28. Someone who does the same thing as another person.

31. Have a lot to do: _____ as a bee.

32. A doorbell ringing: _____ dong!

33. Very common: A _____ a dozen.

DOWN

2. A type of cookie: _____ chip.

3. Go back and forth.

5. Good advice: A _____ to the wise.

7. Money wasted: Money _____ the drain.

9. Exaggerate a problem: Make a _____ out of a molehill.

11. A person who puts out blazes.

12. Go to bed: _____ the hay.

13. Fast and intense instruction: A _____ course.

16. Bugs and worms: _____ crawlies.

17. Gets you angry: Makes your _____ boil.

18. Oil, coal, or gasoline: A _____ fuel.

20. An evil woman: A _____ witch.

24. The three Rs: Reduce, reuse, and _____.

25. Noise from a clock: _____ tock.

27. Something you write to your sweetheart: A _____ letter.

28. A Christmas treat: A _____ cane.

29. A stingy person: A _____ -pincher.

30. Run away: _____ tail.

1. A book about the life of someone.
3. The story is _____ during a war.
6. A story about aliens or robots: _____ fiction.
7. What happens in a book or story.
8. A love story.
9. What the characters say to each other.
14. Books about stories that were made up.
15. A genre of story that contains dragons, knights, fairies, and giants.
17. A book-length story.
19. A formal way to say "the bad guy."
20. A kind of book with cartoons that many kids enjoy.
23. A formal way to say "the main character."
24. A person who draws pictures for a book.
25. A story in which a detective tries to uncover who committed a crime.

DOWN

2. The setting (time) for historical fiction stories.
4. The name of a book.
5. The main character.
7. The story takes _____ in the future.
8. How the main conflict is solved.
10. The most important character: The _____ character.
11. A person who writes a book.
12. The problems the characters face in a story.
13. A story about cowboys in the Wild West.
15. The setting (time) for many science fiction stories.
16. Books about real people and events.
18. A person who is in a story.
19. A story about pirates, treasure seekers, or explorers.
20. A section of a story.
21. A relatively unimportant character: A _____ character.
22. The exciting finish to a story.
23. A story that is acted on a stage.

🔍 All on a Theme

ACROSS

1. A person who has been killed or wounded in a war.
3. Someone who commits a crime.
5. A person who shows new fashion designs.
6. Somebody who loves his or her country.
7. A person who investigates a crime.
9. Somebody who works on a ship.
11. Someone who finds out secrets for his or her country.
12. Somebody who creates new machines or products.
15. A person who studies history.
18. A person who studies ancient life forms.
20. A person who discovers new places.
22. Somebody who acts in movies: A movie _____.
23. A person who has a child.
24. A person who wanders around without having a permanent home.
25. Somebody who flees a war or a natural disaster.

DOWN

1. A person who tells jokes for a living.
2. A person who does not belong to the military.
4. Someone who explores outer space.
6. A person who walks on the street (as opposed to drives in a car).
8. Someone who is a member of a country.
10. A person who has seen a crime.
13. A person who is captured by criminals or terrorists.
14. Someone who has suffered from a crime.
16. A person who predicts your future: A fortune-_____.
17. A person who studies space.
19. A child who doesn't have any parents.
21. Someone who attacks ships at sea.

1. An animal that gives milk to its young and has live birth.
4. A group of wolves or coyotes.
6. An animal that has feathers and lays eggs.
7. Something a bird lays.
9. A six-legged animal with three body parts.
11. A group of cows or wildebeest.
12. A part of a dog that wags.
15. An animal that eats both plants and animals.
16. A thick layer of hair that many mammals have.
18. A thick layer of fat that many arctic animals have.
20. One thread of a food web. (4,5)
22. A bear's or lion's feet.
23. Some animals _____ during the winter when there is little food.
25. Sharp teeth that snakes and other animals have.
28. Something that turtles have that protects them.
31. The place where an animal lives, gets food, and finds shelter.
32. Something fish and tadpoles use to breathe.
33. Something that elephants and walruses use to protect themselves.

DOWN

2. _____ animals are animals that live in the oceans.
3. Something that covers a bird's body.
4. An animal that is hunted by other animals.
5. An animal that eats other animals.
8. _____ animals are animals that do not exist anymore.
10. _____ animals are at risk of becoming extinct.
13. An animal that eats plants.
14. _____ animals are animals that are active at night.
16. The relationships between predator and prey in a community. (4,3)
17. Some animals _____ great distances as the seasons change.
19. Animals with fins, gills, and scales.
21. Sharp things found at the end of some animals' fingers and toes.
24. A lizard, snake, or turtle.
26. Something that covers the skin of many fish and reptiles.
27. Something animals use to fly.
29. Hard, pointy body parts on the heads of some animals such as bulls.
30. Something mammals and reptiles use to breathe.

🔍 *All on a Theme*

ACROSS

1. Go straight to the bottom: _____ like a stone.

2. Keep an eye on someone: _____ someone like a hawk.

4. Fast asleep: _____ like a light.

6. Happy and healthy: _____ like a million bucks.

8. Sneaky: As _____ as a fox.

10. Very dark in color: As _____ as coal.

11. Completely calm: As _____ as a cucumber.

13. Solid: As _____ as rock.

15. Clever: As _____ as a tack.

16. Simple: As _____ as ABC.

18. Very similar: Like two _____ in a pod.

20. Stay away from something: _____ something like the plague.

22. Can't see a thing: As _____ as a bat.

23. Not dirty at all: As _____ as a whistle.

24. Ancient: As _____ as the hills.

26. Not a lot in common: As _____ as night and day.

28. Not damp at all: As _____ as a bone.

30. Nice to look at: As _____ as a picture.

32. Quiet: As _____ as the grave.

33. Well-behaved: As _____ as gold.

DOWN

1. Won't change your mind: As _____ as a mule.

3. Sob a lot: _____ like a baby.

5. Can't hold water: _____ like a sieve.

6. Squashed: As _____ as a pancake.

7. Very ill: As _____ as a dog.

8. Nice to touch: As _____ as silk.

9. Hard to wake up: _____ like a log.

12. A winter color: As _____ as snow.

14. Nothing to hold you down: As _____ as a bird.

15. Easy to notice: _____ _____ like a sore thumb. (5,3)

17. Go around quickly: _____ like wildfire.

19. Hard to grab: As _____ as an eel.

21. Can't touch the bottom: As _____ as the ocean.

23. Quite chilly: As _____ as ice.

25. Not living: As _____ as a doornail.

27. Not much appetite: _____ like a bird.

29. Know what someone is thinking: _____ someone like a book.

31. Sprint: _____ like the wind.

Fixed Phrases

72 About a Country

1. An agreement between two countries. Hint: It begins with T.
6. A rule that people must obey.
7. A line that separates two countries.
10. Sell goods to another country.
11. The branch of the military that guards the nation's soil.
12. A tax that is placed on imported goods.
13. Spanish, French, or Chinese.
14. A building that countries maintain in other countries.
15. The people who prevent crime in a country.
16. A person who works in a court and makes decisions regarding the law.
21. A document your country gives you to prove your nationality.
24. Buy goods from another country.
26. The country a person is from.
27. A person who is a member of a country.
28. The branch of the military that guards a nation's waters.
29. The exchange of goods between countries.

DOWN

2. A country's land.
3. The organization of people who run the country.
4. A military friendship agreement between two countries.
5. The people who put out fires.
8. The main city of a country.

9. A document you need to enter a country.
15. The leader of many democratic nations.
17. A person who negotiates with other countries.
18. The number of people living in a country.
19. A person who loves his or her country.

20. A person who moves into a country.
22. A place where people can seek justice.
23. The branch of the military that guards a nation's skies. (3,5)
25. Money the government collects from citizens and businesses.

All on a Theme

ACROSS

1. Say bad things about someone: _____ somebody down.

3. Do poorly on a test: _____ a test.

4. Start a business: _____ into business.

6. Dirty your house: _____ a mess.

7. Greet someone: _____ hello.

8. Get a satisfactory mark: _____ a test.

9. Do what you said you would: _____ a promise.

11. Give up: _____ in the towel.

12. Delay something to give yourself more time: _____ time.

13. Steal: _____ a crime.

16. Do your share of work: _____ your weight.

19. Take your medicine: _____ your doctor's advice.

20. Say things that aren't true: _____ lies.

23. Sit down: _____ a seat.

24. Stop someone: _____ in someone's way.

25. Know that someone is trying to deceive you: _____ through somebody.

26. Have no contact with a friend: _____ touch.

28. Stop something sinister: _____ the world.

DOWN

1. Make music: _____ an instrument.

2. Tell somebody something the person didn't know: _____ the news.

4. Donate: _____ to charity.

5. Surprise someone: _____ someone off guard.

6. Arrive at the station late: _____ the train.

7. Fire a weapon: _____ a gun.

8. Request a product: _____ an order.

10. Give money to your landlord: _____ the rent.

11. Say something that gets a strong emotional response: _____ a nerve.

14. Fib: _____ a lie.

15. Stop talking about something: _____ the subject.

17. Think you are better than someone: _____ down on a person.

18. Make trouble: _____ problems.

19. Learn something: _____ out something.

21. Take care of children: _____ a family.

22. Tell someone a truth that person didn't want to hear: _____ somebody's bubble.

23. Speak frankly about something: _____ turkey.

27. Pay someone a compliment: _____ highly of someone.

Collocation Awareness

74 The Economy

1. A tax that is levied on imports.
3. How much of a good people want to buy.
6. A place where products are made.
8. Sell goods to another country.
13. Everybody is making money: Business is _____ .
14. The opposite of profit.
15. The industry that includes planting crops.
19. The amount that prices rise over time.
22. The industry that includes extracting metal ore.
23. Money that the government collects from citizens.
24. Trade without any tariffs: _____ trade.
27. Basic materials from which something is manufactured: _____ materials.
28. How much of one country's money you get for another country's money: The _____ rate.
29. A situation in which workers refuse to work.
30. Things you buy and sell.

DOWN

2. Buy goods from another country.
4. A situation where there is only one seller.
5. The number of people not working: The _____ rate.
7. A person who buys goods or services.
9. Money you earn above what you spend in a business.

10. A time when the economy is bad.
11. The money used to start a business.
12. How much money you owe.
14. Money you borrow from someone.
16. How much money you earn.
17. A group of workers who get together to protect their rights.

18. A country's money.
20. A good that is sold to the consumer: _____ product.
21. Extra money you pay when you borrow money.
25. A place where people save their money.
26. The lowest amount that an employer can pay an employee: The minimum _____ .

🔍 All on a Theme

ACROSS

1. Everest, Fuji, or Kilimanjaro.
2. Beef, pork, or poultry.
4. Pianist, violinist, or guitarist.
7. Sight, touch, or hearing.
9. Frog, toad, or salamander.
10. Pine, oak, or maple.
11. Emperor, czar, or king.
15. Almond, pistachio, or pecan.
16. Chess, checkers, or Monopoly.
17. North, east, or south.
21. Hammer, saw, or shovel.
24. French, Spanish, or Chinese.
25. Sofas, tables, and chairs.
26. Three, five, or nine.
27. Copper, iron, or gold.
28. Pacific, Atlantic, or Indian.
29. *Moby Dick, Huckleberry Finn,* or *Harry Potter and the Sorcerer's Stone.*
30. March, May, or August.

DOWN

1. Human, whale, or bat.
2. Troll, goblin, or vampire.
3. Snake, turtle, or lizard.
5. Oregano, chili, or pepper.
6. Europe, Asia, or Africa.
8. Prince, duke, or baron.
12. Amazon, Nile, or Mississippi.
13. Mars, Jupiter, or Saturn.
14. Radio, television, and newspapers.
18. Red, blue, or green.
19. Heart, liver, or stomach.
20. Carrot, onion, or lettuce.
22. Mountain, valley, or plain.
23. Madrid, Beijing, or Moscow.
25. Rose, tulip, or daffodil.

Word Skills 📝

76 Family

3. Short for mother.
4. All of the cousins and siblings around the same age.
6. A male parent.
9. The sister of your mother or father.
10. Your aunt's or uncle's child.
12. Short for grandfather.
14. Your spouse's family. (2-4)
17. A family that consists of more than just parents and children: An _____ family.
19. A male child.
21. A cousin, aunt, uncle, or grandparent.
22. A female child.
24. Your child's child.
25. A male sibling.

DOWN

1. A female spouse.
2. Your mom and dad.
3. A female parent.
4. Your mother's or father's father.
5. A child who has lost his or her parents.
7. Agree to raise someone else's child.

8. A male spouse.
11. Your mother's or father's mother.
12. Short for grandmother.
13. A husband or wife.
15. A female sibling.
16. A time when people get married.

18. Your grandmother's mother: Your _____-grandmother.
20. A family that consists of parents and children: A _____ family.
22. Short for father.
23. The brother of your mother or father.

🔍 All on a Theme

ACROSS

1. The time of day when many people eat dinner.
4. Someone who catches criminals: A police _____ .
8. A thing that spiders make.
9. A part of a ship where people walk.
11. A part of a plant that can make new plants.
13. A place where criminals are put on trial.
14. A thing that people use to separate solids and liquids.
15. A place where people drive cars.
16. A domesticated animal that is raised for meat.
19. A piece of furniture that many people can sit on.
21. Something you draw.
22. A thing that takes pictures.
24. A place where crime fighters work. (6,7)
26. A holiday when people send cards and chocolates to people they love: _____ Day.
28. An insect that makes honey.
29. Something people watch at home.
30. A person that says the news.
33. A person who acts in movies.
34. A place where many shops are gathered under one roof: A shopping _____ .
36. A part of your body that you use to hear.
37. A bird that farmers raise.
38. Body parts you brush.

DOWN

2. A part of your body that you use to see.
3. A part of your body that you use to smell.
4. A bird that is active at night.
5. A part of a fish that it uses to move.
6. Somebody who builds houses: A _____ worker.
7. A piece of furniture that people sleep on.
8. A forest animal that hunts in packs.
10. A holiday when people hang stockings and give gifts.
12. Something people use to fix mistakes made by a pencil.
13. A person who cooks food.
16. A thing that people use to boil eggs.
17. A large primate that lives in Africa.
18. A thing that you can pedal.
20. A place where many families live together in the same building.
23. A thing that you answer when it rings.
25. Somebody who sews clothes.
26. Someone who helps sick animals.
27. Something people use when they sew.
31. A device that people listen to.
32. A part of a plant that gathers water.
35. An insect that lives in a colony.

2. A place where people grow flowers and other plants.
5. An insect that pollinates flowers.
7. A sharp part on some plant stems.
8. A colorful part of a plant that blooms.
10. Another word for dirt.
11. A flower that begins with R.
14. A tree that is famous for its red leaves in autumn.
16. A plant found in the desert.
19. Something people use to water the garden.
20. Something that plants need to make food.
21. A part of a plant that gathers water from the soil.
22. The part of a pine tree that contains seeds.
24. The leaves of a pine tree.
25. A conifer that begins with P.
26. A product that comes from trees.
28. The type of plant that grapes and pumpkins grow on.

DOWN

1. A part of a plant that makes food out of sunlight.
3. The seed of an oak tree.
4. An almond, a walnut, or a pecan.
5. A flower before it blooms.
6. An apple, a peach, or a pear.
9. A plant that is just breaking through the soil.
10. A part of a plant that holds the plant up.
12. Another word for flower.
13. The type of plant that forms your lawn.
15. A sticky powder that helps make seeds.
17. The season when leaves change color.
18. Something people use to dig.
19. Gather the crops.
22. Plants grown by farmers for food.
23. A plant that people don't want in their gardens.
26. Something plants need to grow.
27. A tree that begins with O.

Q **All on a Theme**

ACROSS

3. Love someone even though the person has faults: Love someone _____ and all.

5. Get offended: Take something the wrong _____.

7. Help you remember: Jog your _____.

8. Ignore someone: Give someone the cold _____.

10. Say exactly what the problem is: Hit the _____ on the head.

12. Cause trouble in a peaceful situation: Rock the _____.

14. A warning to change your behavior: A wake-up _____.

15. A problem you no longer need to worry about: A _____ off of your shoulders.

16. In good times and bad times: Through thick and _____.

18. Do something without a plan: Play it by _____.

19. Feel sick: Feel under the _____.

20. Get angry: Lose your _____.

22. Start something too soon: Jump the _____.

24. Do something bad: Be _____ to no good.

25. Survive a difficult situation: Weather a _____.

26. Get something to eat: Grab a _____.

DOWN

1. Watch something carefully: Keep an _____ on it.

2. Have someone be very pleased with you: Be in someone's good _____.

3. Stop your bad behavior: Mend your _____.

4. Try to do something: Give something a _____.

5. A person who seems harmless: A _____ in sheep's clothing.

6. A very light punishment for your crime: A slap on the _____.

7. Decide to do something: _____ up your mind.

9. Do something unpleasant that has to be done: Bite the _____.

10. In a very remote location without many people: In the middle of _____.

11. Tell a lie to play a joke on a person: Pull someone's _____.

12. Find out what really happened: Get to the _____ of something.

13. A small portion of the actual amount: The tip of the _____.

17. Do something very risky: Skate on thin _____.

20. Look awkward: Stand out like a sore _____.

21. Try not to stand out or get noticed: Keep a low _____.

23. Cheap: Costs next to _____.

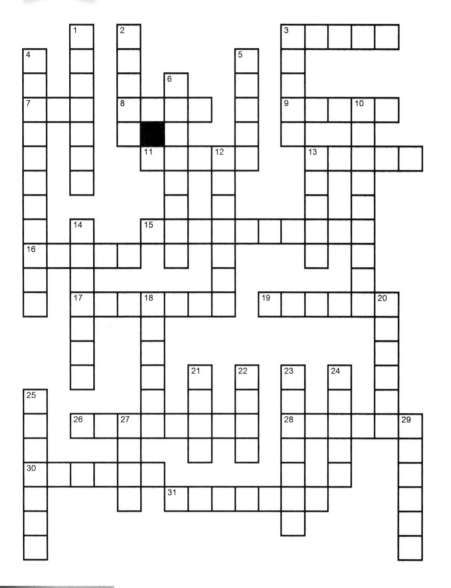

3. Grab your glove and baseball. Let's play _____.

7. A time when you don't work: A day _____.

8. Here's a sketchbook. Go _____ a picture.

9. A recreational activity where you put on an air tank and go underwater: _____ diving.

11. _____ a game on TV.

13. Hobby: Make a _____ airplane or ship.

15. Keep a _____ of coins or stamps.

16. A musical instrument with black and white keys.

17. Take a tent and go _____.

19. Go _____ in the mountains.

26. A sport where you hit a ball with a bat.

28. A winter recreational activity done on a mountain slope.

30. Borrow a racket and play _____.

31. A game where you get strikes and spares.

DOWN

1. There are some good waves. Grab your board and let's go _____.

2. Something with an ace, king, and queen.

3. A game with a king, a queen, a rook, and pawns.

4. The activity of taking pictures.

5. Get a tan at the _____.

6. A time when students don't have to go to school.

10. A game where you hit a birdie over a net.

12. The activity of riding a bike.

13. Listen to _____ on the radio.

14. A recreational activity where you move your body to the music.

18. Put the pieces of a _____ together.

20. Plant some flowers in your _____.

21. _____ a book or a magazine.

22. Go for a _____ in the park.

23. Bring some hooks and bait when you go _____.

24. Grab a brush. Let's _____ a picture.

25. A winter recreational activity done on ice.

27. Go for a _____ in the pool.

29. A musical instrument with six strings.

🔍 All on a Theme

ACROSS

1. Check your _____ to find out the time.
2. Wear a _____ to cut down on heat use.
5. Climb a _____ to reach something.
7. Turn up the _____ to hear the TV better.
9. Use a _____ to wipe the table.
11. Put a _____ on your hook to catch a fish.
12. Set your _____ to wake up.
13. Ride a _____ to cut down on gas consumption.
15. Open a _____ to let some air in.
16. Go to the _____ to work out.
19. Use your _____ to make a purchase. (6,4)
20. Use a _____ to water the garden.
22. Mix yellow and _____ to make orange.
23. Open the _____ to let someone in.
25. Call the _____ to report a crime.
26. Mix yellow and _____ to make green.
27. Use some _____ to wash your clothes.
29. Wear a _____ to protect your head.
30. Use a _____ to blow your nose.
31. Wait in _____ to buy a ticket.

DOWN

1. Use a _____ to carry your cash.
3. Use an _____ to withdraw some cash.
4. Call a _____ to fix your sink.
6. Check a _____ to find out what a word means.
8. Go to the _____ to borrow some books.
10. Raise your _____ to ask a question.
13. Use a _____ to paint something.
14. Use a _____ to organize your files.
17. Take some _____ to get over a cold.
18. Go to the _____ to mail a parcel. (4,6)
21. Get a _____ to earn some money.
23. See a _____ to get a cavity filled.
24. Stretch your _____ to prevent injury when you exercise.
27. Go on a _____ to lose some weight.
28. Send an _____ to contact someone. (1-4)

82 Personalities

1. A _____ person is someone who says, "Please," and "Thank you."
4. A _____ person is someone who has lots of experience and knowledge.
6. The opposite of lazy.
9. A _____ person is someone who keeps his or her house clean.
12. Another word for brave.
13. A _____ person is someone who doesn't keep a clean house.
17. A _____ person is someone who doesn't work very hard.
19. An _____ person is someone who thinks good things will happen in the future.
20. A _____ person is someone who is nice to other people.
21. An _____ person is someone who has high goals.
24. A _____ person is someone who is not afraid to do something.
26. A _____ person is someone who thinks of other people and does things for them. Hint: It begins with C.
27. A _____ person is someone who wants to have everything.
28. A _____ person is someone who makes people laugh.

DOWN

2. Another word for considerate. Hint: It begins with TH.
3. A _____ person is nice to people he or she meets. Hint: It begins with F.
5. Another word for outgoing.
7. A _____ person is someone who is giving and sharing.
8. If you have a sense of _____, then you know what is funny.

10. A _____ person is someone who is always on time. Hint: It begins with P.
11. A _____ person is someone who thinks bad things will happen in the future.
14. A _____ person is someone who feels uncomfortable meeting new people.
15. A _____ person is someone you can depend on.

16. An _____ person is someone who likes to meet people.
18. An _____ person is someone who doesn't lie.
22. A _____ person is someone who doesn't like to spend any money.
23. Another word for smart.
25. The opposite of polite.

All on a Theme

ACROSS

1. A planet that begins with M.
2. A type of meat that begins with P.
4. A farm animal that begins with G.
6. A shape that begins with C.
7. An aquatic animal that ends with SH.
9. A month that ends with Y.
14. A reptile that begins with I.
15. A tree that begins with O.
17. An insect that begins with G.
22. A metal that begins with G.
23. A bird that ends with W.
24. A continent that begins with E.
26. A forest animal that ends with X.
28. A form of transportation that begins with T.
31. A marine animal that begins with O.
32. An ocean that begins with A.
35. A type of meat that begins with B.
36. A colorful bird that begins with P.

DOWN

1. A month that begins with M.
2. A tree that begins with P.
3. A hot drink that ends with EE.
5. A continent that begins with A.
8. A season that ends with NG.
9. A drink that begins with M.
10. A color that ends with W.
11. A set of human organs that begins with L.
12. A flower that begins with T.
13. A flower that begins with R.
16. A farm animal that begins with P.
18. A type of media that begins with R.
19. A number that ends with X.
20. A fruit that begins with O.
21. An ocean that begins with P.
25. A color that ends with K.
27. A drink that begins with J.
28. A part of your hand that ends with B.
29. A fruit that begins with A.
30. A piece of furniture that begins with CH.
31. A bird that begins with O.
33. An insect that begins with A.
34. A hot drink that begins with T.

Banking and Finance

ACROSS

1. Return borrowed money: _____ off a debt.
3. The amount of money you owe.
5. A card that lets you buy things with money directly from your bank: _____ card.
7. Amount of money you earn.
8. A person who gives money to a company in hope of future profits.
9. To open an account, you have to _____ out some forms.
11. A person who serves you at a bank.
12. A machine used to withdraw cash.
13. A plan for how you use your money.
14. A regular income you get when you retire.
17. Money that you carry on you.
19. Money that is lent to someone.
20. Something banks do before they give you a loan: A credit _____.
24. Money you earn above your expenses.
25. Money to spend on whatever you want: Money to _____.
26. Borrow money from the bank: _____ out a loan.
27. Metal money.
28. A special loan for purchasing a house.
29. A regular amount of money returned to the bank to reduce the amount of your loan.
30. Start using a bank: Open an _____.
31. Keep money for an emergency: Save for a _____ day.

DOWN

1. A secret code you use to withdraw money from an ATM.
2. If you are broke, you can _____ money from a friend.
3. Put money into your account.
4. A place where people save money.
6. Money you pay regularly for protection in case of misfortune.
10. The opposite of borrow.
13. The local office of your bank.
15. Passport, birth certificate, or driver's license.
16. How much money is left in your account.
18. The extra money you pay when you borrow money.
21. A country's money.
22. A record of your bank account that is sent to you monthly.
23. If you are _____, then you have no money to spend.
28. Something people use to buy things.

🔍 **All on a Theme**

ACROSS

3. Someone who fixes cars.

5. A thing that birds lay.

6. Somebody who puts out fires.

10. A time when students celebrate finishing school.

11. Things that you brush before bed.

13. Something people play.

14. A place where people park their cars: A parking _____.

15. A bicycle part you use to steer.

17. A bird that is active at night.

19. A pet that has whiskers.

20. A branch of mathematics that deals with shapes and angles.

22. The season when leaves change color.

24. A branch of the military that protects a country's land.

26. A piece of jewelry that you wear on your wrist.

29. A place where people live.

31 A person who tells you the news.

33. Something you turn on when it's dark.

DOWN

1. A time when very little rain falls and plants die.

2. A place where people order food.

4. Something people drive.

6. Something people use to see in the dark.

7. A body part you use to touch.

8. A place where people from out of town sleep.

9. A time when people vote.

12. A thing that people wear on their heads.

16. A thing that people use to sweep.

18. An African animal that has a mane.

19. A place where people drink coffee.

21 Somebody who teaches children.

23. A thing kids use to catch bugs.

25. Something you catch with a hook.

26. A mammal that can fly.

27. A person who cooks food.

28. A body part you use to hear.

30. A place that has many stores: A shopping _____.

32. Something people watch at home.

86 Ancient Civilization and Early Humans

1. Things that happened long ago: _____ history.
4. The study of the past using written documents.
6. A system of writing where the symbols represent sounds.
8. The movement of people from one place to another.
9. Hammurabi's Code: An _____ for an eye.
11. Artifacts made from baked clay that were used to hold goods.
12. An important early metal made by mixing copper and tin.
14. A two-wheeled wagon that was sometimes used in war.
16. A person who was believed to have magical powers in some tribes.
17. A person who performs religious services.
22. The growing of crops.
23. The process of changing wild animals into animals raised by people.
27. A hard metal that eventually replaced bronze in weapon making.
28. What occurs when too much rain causes rivers to overflow.
29. A precious metal used to make jewelry.
30. A region where many early civilizations existed: The _____ Crescent.

DOWN

2. Something farmers grow.
3. A ruler in ancient Egypt.
5. An ancient trade route that extended from China to the Roman Empire: The _____ Road.
6. A system for bringing water to a city.
7. The exchange of goods between people.
10. A person who travels from place to place without having a fixed home.
13. The civilization that built the pyramids at Giza.
15. A system for bringing water to crops.
16. Extra of something (like crops, for example).
18. A person who could write.
19. Something made by humans that archaeologists study.
20. A system of expressing language on stone, clay, papyrus, or paper.
21. A large stone structure where Egyptians buried their rulers.
24. An early material for making tools.
25. The river where Egyptian civilization was based.
26. A _____ of laws.

All on a Theme

ACROSS

1. A dirty hit: _____ the belt.

4. A Halloween greeting: _____ or-treat!

7. Revenge: _____ for tat.

8. Bugs and worms: _____ crawlies.

9. A doorbell ringing: _____ dong!

11. Exaggerate a problem: Make a _____ out of a molehill.

12. A bakery purchase: A _____ donuts.

13. A place to find ghosts: A _____ house.

14. Sound from a clock: _____ tock.

16. Go to sleep: _____ the hay.

17. Causes you to be mad: Makes your _____ boil.

18. Something you write to your sweetheart: A _____ letter.

19. Fast and intense instruction: A _____ course.

20. A stocking stuffer: A _____ cane.

21. A person who puts out blazes.

26. A friendly greeting: A _____ welcome.

27. A person who steals your wallet.

28. Be careful: _____ before you leap!

29. A stingy person: A _____-pincher.

30. Common: A _____ a dozen.

31. The whole day: From _____ to dusk.

DOWN

1. Can't see at all: _____ as a bat.

2. A place for cowboys: The _____ West.

3. A Thanksgiving treat: _____ pie.

5. Find ways to save money: _____ corners.

6. Nice to look at: _____ as a picture.

7. Something that's hard to say: A _____ twister.

10. Carbon dioxide: A _____ gas.

11. A person who introduces couples.

12. Money wasted: Money _____ the drain.

13. Wait! _____ your horses!

15. A dairy product: _____ cheese.

21. Oil, coal, or gasoline: A _____ fuel.

22. A path for trains.

23. Have more important things to do: Have bigger _____ to fry.

24. Assist someone: Lend a _____ hand.

25. Someone who does the same thing as another person.

26. An evil sorceress: A _____ witch.

88 Raw Materials and Natural Resources

4. A material that comes from trees.
5. Energy that comes from the sun.
6. A raw material used to make wine.
7. A metal alloy made from copper and tin.
9. A precious metal used to make jewelry.
11. A material that can be used to change the color of hair or cloth.
12. A black rock that is burned to generate heat.
13. A material used to make toys and bottles.
17. Any material used in cooking.
19. Anything that people use that comes from the earth: A _____ resource.
20. A black liquid used as fuel.
21. Something people build to generate hydroelectric power.
23. A person who grows crops.
26. A place where people dig for metal ore.
27. A place where products are made.
28. A raw material used to make tires and balloons.
29. A clothing material that comes from animal skin.

DOWN

1. A material used to make windows and mirrors.
2. A metal used to make electrical wires.
3. A hard metal with magnetic properties.
4. A material used to make sweaters that comes from sheep.
6. People _____ electricity using solar and wind energy.
8. The materials used to make other things: _____ materials.

10. A person who raises cattle or sheep.
12. A clothing material that comes from a plant.
13. A place where electricity is generated. (5,5)
14. A hard material early humans used to make tools.
15. Things like iron, gold, or copper.
16. A hard, red material used to make walls.

18. A precious metal used to make jewelry.
20. Rock that contains metal.
22. A person who digs metal ore from the ground.
24. A smooth, shiny, white stone that is used in buildings.
25. A metal alloy made from carbon and iron.
26. Something used to make dairy products.

All on a Theme

ACROSS

1. If you _____ **into** somebody, you meet that person unexpectedly.
3. Make sure you _____ **out of** your account when you are finished.
5. Did you _____ **in on** the meeting?
7. The client called just as I was about to _____ **out** for lunch.
9. My doctor told me to _____ **down on** eating meat.
10. They really _____ it **off** from the first time they met.
12. They _____ **up** the tent at the campsite.
13. I bought that yesterday, so you can _____ it **off** our list.
15. It was a good offer, but I told them I had to _____ it **over** before I could decide.
17. _____ **off** the lights before you go to bed.
18. If you _____ something **up**, you start to talk about that topic.
19. This room is a mess! Please _____ **away** your toys before our guests arrive.
21. If you don't stop talking on your phone, they will _____ you **out of** the theater.
23. Drive slow or you'll _____ **up** in the hospital.
25. I have a report due in the morning, so I have to _____ **up** all night and do it.

DOWN

1. Which team are you going to _____ **for**?
2. I've been away all week, so I want to _____ **up on** the news.
3. I'll _____ you **in on** a secret.
4. Even after everybody advised against it, you are going to _____ **ahead with** your plan.
5. Did you _____ **to** your diet today?
6. Do you recycle cans? Or do you just _____ them **away**?
8. If you **take** _____ **in** something, you participate.
11. He wears really bright clothes that make him _____ **out** in a crowd.
14. Could you _____ **by** the store on the way home and pick up some milk?
16. I have to _____ **out** these pamphlets to people in the crowd.
18. They were dating, but they had a fight and decided to _____ **up**.
20. You should _____ **on** those pants before you buy them.
22. You have to _____ **out** of the hotel before 11:00.
24. If you _____ something **over**, you redo it.
26. They are identical! I can't _____ them **apart**.

Fixed Phrases

Word Skills Hodgepodge 1

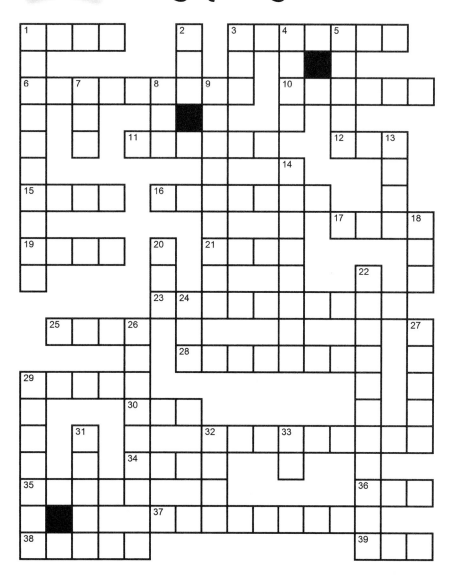

1. The antonym of new (as in a new car).
3. The opposite of sick.
6. The opposite of alike.
10. A reptile that begins with I.
11. A synonym of reply.
12. A mammal that begins with B.
15. A synonym of skinny.
16. A planet that begins with J.
17. Another word for enjoy.
19. Another word for close.
21. A tree that begins with P.
23. A berry that begins with S.
25. A synonym of aid.
28. The antonym of stingy.
29. Another word for clever.
30. An insect that begins with A.
32. The antonym of safe.
34. A continent that begins with A.
35. The opposite of quiet.
36. A farm animal that begins with P.
37. Another word for costly.
38. A synonym of foe.
39. The opposite of cooked.

DOWN

1. A synonym of comprehend.
2. The opposite of live.
3. The opposite of cold.
4. The opposite of humid.
5. A part of your hand that ends with B.
7. Another word for repair.
8. The opposite of walk.
9. A type of media that begins with N.
13. Another word for chat.
14. A synonym of recall.
18. Another word for finish.
20. A form of transportation that begins with B.
22. An insect that begins with G.
24. Another word for pull.
26. The antonym of take out (as in take out your books). (3,4)
27. Human organs that begins with L.
29. Another word for weird.
31. The antonym of lower.
32. Another way to say "a little wet."
33. The antonym of come.

Word Skills

ACROSS

2. The past tense of win.
3. The plural form of this.
5. The past participle of bite.
8. The past tense of stand.
9. The past tense of throw.
10. The plural form of foot.
12. The past participle of swell.
13. The past tense of hear.
14. The past participle of ring.
17. The plural form of child.
21. The past tense of understand.
23. The past tense of dig.
24. The past participle of hide.
26. The superlative form of little.
27. The past tense of make.
29. The past tense of sleep.
31. The past participle of speak.
33. The past tense of eat.
34. The past participle of write.
35. The past participle of take.

DOWN

1. The past tense of bite.
2. The past tense of go.
4. The past participle of shine.
6. The past participle of throw.
7. The plural form of tooth.
10. The superlative form of far.
11. The past participle of teach.
12. The past participle of strike.
15. The plural form of man.
16. The past participle of bring.
18. The comparative form of bad.
19. The past participle of find.
20. The past tense of fall.
22. The past tense of do.
23. The past tense of drink.
25. The past tense of draw.
28. The past participle of eat.
30. The past tense of take.
31. The past tense of see.
32. The past tense of run.

Word Skills

4. Change from liquid to solid.
9. A theory that says animals change over time.
10. Liquid rock inside the Earth.
11. Information that you gather.
13. How fast velocity changes.
16. A tool used to separate solids and liquids.
19. A hot, glowing ball of gas in space.
20. A scientific way to say "push apart."
21. Show that a theory is wrong.
23. Your genetic code.
25. How much space something occupies.
28. A path that electricity follows.
31. A scientific way to say "pull together."
32. Material like iron, copper, or gold.
33. Explode like a volcano.
34. A push or a pull (like gravity or friction).
35. Write data down.

DOWN

1. The force that slows down moving things that are touching.
2. Study something in depth: Do _____.
3. The planets _____ around the sun.
5. Anything that has mass and occupies space.
6. Energy from motion: _____ energy.
7. The state of matter that maintains its shape.

8. A ball of ice and dust in space.
12. A rock floating in space.
14. The state of matter that flows.
15. An imaginary line that something turns on.
16. What remains of an animals or a plant.
17. Change from solid to liquid.
18. Show that a theory is correct.
22. A material that does not conduct heat or electricity well.

24. A form of energy that makes things hot.
26. A scientific way to say that an animal no longer exists.
27. See how big, wide, hot, or heavy something is.
29. Another way to say "turn on an axis."
30. An explanation for why something happens.
32. A measure of how much matter something has.

🔍 All on a Theme

ACROSS

1. Your main source of income: Your bread and _____.

3. Things on your feet: Shoes and _____.

4. Your whole body: From head to _____.

5. What a sentry asks: Friend or _____?

6. Hunting tools: Bow and _____.

8. In a safe place: Under lock and _____.

10. Everywhere: From top to _____.

13. Wild West poster: Wanted dead or _____.

14. Things to write with: Pen and _____.

16. Utensils: Knife and _____.

17. Royalty: King and _____.

18. Parents: Mom and _____.

20. A good way to finish: Save the best for _____.

22. A marriage vow: For better or for _____.

23. Things that break bones: Sticks and _____.

25. Hawaiian pizza: Ham and _____.

27. Become wealthy: Go from rags to _____.

29. Compromise: Give and _____.

30. The whole universe: Heaven and _____.

31. An American breakfast: Bacon and _____.

DOWN

2. A Halloween greeting: Trick-or- _____!

3. A children's game: Hide-and- _____.

5. Good times or bad: Feast or _____.

7. An old photograph: Black-and- _____.

9. The whole time: From beginning to _____.

10. Children: Girls and _____.

11. Fight as hard as you can: Fight tooth and _____.

12. Incentives to do something: The stick and the _____.

15. What the law concerns: Crime and _____.

18. The whole night: From dusk to _____.

19. A heavy rain: Cats and _____.

21. Siblings: Brother and _____.

24. Why something happened: Cause and _____.

25. The setting of a story: The time and _____.

26. A link in the food chain: Predator and _____.

28. Weighing an argument: Listing the pros and _____.

94 Synonyms 2

ACROSS

1. Another word for fortunate.
3. A synonym of despise.
5. A synonym of fragment.
8. Another word for summit.
9. A synonym of tidy.
10. Another word for infant.
12. A synonym of giggle.
14. Another word for seat.
17. Another word for error.
19. Another word for close.
20. Another word for center.
21. Another way to say "a little wet."
23. Another word for arrive.
24. Another word for shove.
26. Another word for shout.
29. Another word for weird.
32. Another word for mad.
33. A synonym of rapid.
34. Another word for costly.
35. Another word for ill.
36. A synonym of harm.

DOWN

2. A synonym of insane.
4. Another word for garbage.
5. A synonym of forecast.
6. A synonym of wicked.
7. Another word for finish.
11. Another word for construct.
12. Another way to say "jump far."
13. A synonym of cautious.
15. A synonym of assault.
16. A synonym of recall.
18. A synonym of foe.
21. Another word for ruin.
22. A synonym of persuade.
25. Another word for pull.
27. A synonym of position.
28. Another way to say "talk quietly."
29. A synonym of recommend.
30. A synonym of simple (to do).
31. A synonym of locate.
33. Another word for repair.

Word Skills

ACROSS

1. A heavy snowstorm.
2. A precious metal.
4. A stinging insect.
5. A sour fruit.
7. A spicy vegetable. (5,6)
10. A leafy vegetable.
11. A flying mammal.
13. A prickly plant.
14. A tall building.
16. A legless reptile
17. A two-wheeled vehicle.
18. An eight-legged sea creature.
21. An old story.
22. A tall person.
23. A fast run.
24. A wandering tribesman.

DOWN

1. A sandy shore.
2. A strong wind.
3. A heavy rain.
4. A light wind.
6. A bloodsucking insect.
7. A one-eyed giant.
8. Frozen water.
9. Liquid rock.
11. A heavy load.
12. A long run.
13. An orange vegetable.
15. A transparent material.
16. An underground train.
17. A large house.
19. A flightless bird.
20. A fire-breathing monster.

ACROSS

2. The antonym of real.
3. Another word for construct.
5. A piece of furniture that begins with T.
7. The opposite of sick.
8. The antonym of crooked.
9. The antonym of deceitful.
11. The antonym of laugh.
12. A fruit that begins with A.
14. A month that ends with Y.
16. A synonym of cautious.
19. A synonym of persuade.
20. The antonym of black.
22. A continent that begins with E.
25. A number that ends with X.
26. The antonym of old.
27. A bird that begins with O.
28. The antonym of safe.
33. A marine animal that begins with O.
36. A synonym of position.
37. Another word for chat.
38. A synonym of fragment.

DOWN

1. A type of meat that begins with B.
2. The opposite of lead (as in lead someone somewhere).
3. The opposite of doubt (as in doubt what somebody says).
4. A vegetable that begins with L.
6. An insect that begins with A.
8. A fruit that begins with S.
10. A synonym of simple (to do).
11. A shape that begins with C.
13. The antonym of put down (as in put down your pencil). (4,2)
15. The opposite of humid.
17. The opposite of cooked.
18. The opposite of pass (as in pass an exam).
21. The opposite of late.
22. Another word for costly.
23. Another word for finish.
24. A synonym of naughty.
25. The opposite of float.
29. A fruit that begins with O.
30. The opposite of long.
31. The opposite of cold.
32. The antonym of freeze.
34. A tree that begins with O.
35. The antonym of new (as in a car).

ACROSS

2. A desert plant with needles.

4. A building with many works of art in it.

6. A building with many stores inside it.

7. A sea creature with stinging tentacles.

11. A sea creature with eight legs.

14. A cat with spots.

16. A long time without rain.

20. A frozen biome with no trees.

22. A building with many homes in it.

23. A piece of paper with locations on it.

25. An animal with a long neck.

26. An animal with long ears.

28. A toy with a long string.

29. A reptile without legs.

30. A building with many books.

DOWN

1. A biome with very little rain.

2. A giant with one eye.

3. A musical instrument with black and white keys.

5. An animal with a long trunk.

8. An animal with gills and fins.

9. An animal with eight legs.

10. A chair with no back.

12. A mythical woman with snakes in her hair.

13. A reptile with a shell on its back.

15. A child without parents.

16. A snack with a hole in it.

17. A horse with a horn.

18. A sea creature with five legs.

19. A pet with whiskers.

21. A biome with lots of precipitation and many trees.

24. A toy with many pieces that fit together.

25. A musical instrument with six strings.

27. An animal with feathers.

ACROSS

2. We need to talk. Why don't we _____ **together** at 4:00?
4. _____ **up** your bags. It's time to go.
6. If you _____ someone **off**, you cheat that person.
8. _____ **off** the stove after you are finished cooking.
10. Did you _____ **out** how to solve the problem?
11. _____ **out**! That's dangerous.
13. Make sure you _____ **out of** your account when you are finished.
16. He had really terrible grades, so he decided to _____ **out of** school.
18. My doctor recommended that I _____ **down on** eating meat.
20. I usually _____ **up** at 6:30 A.M.
21. I have a report due in the morning, so I'll probably _____ **up** all night to get it done.
23. Did you _____ **to** your diet today?
25. If you _____ something **up**, you start to talk about it.
27. If you _____ **through** something, you survive a terrible experience.
28. Do you _____ **after** your mom or your dad?

DOWN

1. I used to _____ **around** with him in high school.
2. I decided to _____ them **away** for free.
3. Do you recycle plastic containers? Or do you just _____ them **away**?
5. I've been away so I want to _____ **up** on the news.
7. It's cold outside. Why don't you _____ **on** a coat?
9. If you _____ **out of** something, you have used it up.
10. You need to _____ **out** this form.
12. _____ that **off** the list.
14. The couple began to _____ **apart**, and eventually they broke up.
15. You have to _____ **up to** your problems.
17. Because of the economic downturn, the company began to _____ **off** workers.
19. If you _____ someone **out of** doing something, that means you convince that person not to do it.
22. I have to _____ it **over** before I can decide.
23. They _____ **up** the tent at the campsite.
24. You should _____ **out** the new exhibit at the museum.
26. Are you going to _____ **ahead with** your plan?

 Fixed Phrases

ACROSS

1. Where anybody can see: In _____.
7. Have a similar characteristic: Have something in _____.
8. Not fighting: At _____.
9. Not saying anything: Without a _____.
11. You alone: By _____.
15. At a reduced price: On _____.
16. Not in the port: At _____.
17. Not moving: At _____.
18. Crazy about someone: In _____.
20. As a rule: In _____.
21. Crying: In _____.
22. Where no one can see: In _____.
23. Specifically: In _____.
24. Without meaning to: By _____.
30. (Talk) for a long time: At _____.
31. Not working: Out of _____.
34. Fighting: At _____.
35. Comfortable: At _____.
36. None left in the store: Out of _____.
37. Not late: On _____.

DOWN

2. Prohibited: Off _____.
3. (Know) from memory: By _____.
4. Can be seen: In _____.
5. Nearby: At _____.
6. Working (as a soldier, police officer, or firefighter): On _____.
8. Broken apart: In _____.
10. Intentionally: On _____.
12. Riding: On _____.
13. Accidentally: By _____.
14. Not in a safe situation: In _____.
15. Without anyone knowing: In _____.
19. Consequently: As a _____.
21. Not what we were talking about: Off _____.
22. To be careful: As a _____.
25. Coincidently: By _____.
26. Owing money: In _____.
27. Burning: On _____.
28. Eventually: In due _____.
29. Unemployed: Out of _____.
30. A minimum of: At _____.
32. Not at night: By _____.
33. Can't be grabbed: Out of _____.

100 The Way You Say It

1. Ask for something in a desperate way.

4. Point out someone's faults.

7. What you do if someone asks you a question.

8. Ask somebody to do something for you.

9. Talk excitedly.

10. What you do if you want to know something.

13. Tell someone about a good book, movie, or restaurant that you think the person should see.

16. Say that you didn't do a crime: _____ doing it.

18. Say something in short, highlighting only the important points.

19. Say you won't do something.

21. Say the same thing again but in a different way.

23. Tell someone about danger.

25. Say something that isn't true.

28. Say you don't like something or that something isn't good.

29. Talk loudly.

DOWN

1. Another word for brag.

2. Tell someone all of the good reasons to do something.

3. Say you are the best at something.

5. Say that you will hurt someone.

6. Say the same thing again.

11. Talk quietly.

12. Spread rumors about people.

14. The way a captain tells someone to do something.

15. Say something nice about someone.

17. Use bad language.

20. Say how to do something.

22. Give a clue.

24. Tell someone what he or she should do or what would be good for that person.

26. Another word for yell.

27. Another word for answer.

🔍 *All on a Theme*

ACROSS

1. A monster that drinks blood.
4. A monster wrapped in bandages.
7. Something a witch uses to fly.
8. The month of Halloween.
11. A vampire's bed.
13. A place where ghosts live: _____ house.
14. A pumpkin that has been carved: Jack-o'-_____ .
15. A person who juggles and makes you laugh.
16. Sound like a werewolf.
18. A monster made of bones.
19. Another word for scary.
20. A Halloween bird.
21. A witch, a werewolf, or a zombie.
23. A woman with a black pointy hat.
25. A flying animal.
26. A creature from outer space.
27. A place where people are buried.
28. A witch's laugh.

DOWN

2. A large orange vegetable seen on Halloween.
3. A mechanical person made of metal and wires.
4. Something you color your face with on Halloween.
5. Something you wear on your face on Halloween.
6. A spirit of the dead.
7. A witch's pet. (5,3)
9. Sound like an owl.
10. An animal that makes cobwebs.
12. A monster that howls at the full moon.
13. A Sleepy Hollow ghoul: The _____ Horseman.
15. Something you wear on Halloween.
17. A walking dead person.
20. A Halloween color.
22. A Halloween greeting: _____-or-treat!
24. Something children get on Halloween.
25. A Halloween color.

102 Thanksgiving

1. An event in which bands and people wearing costumes march down the street or ride in floats.
2. A yellow vegetable that was grown by Native Americans.
5. The month of Thanksgiving.
10. _____ thanks for the food we eat.
11. A place where things are baked.
12. A large bird eaten on Thanksgiving.
13. _____ a turkey in the oven.
14. A large dinner celebration.
15. Food you eat the day after Thanksgiving.
18. Another word for thankful.
20. An odd-shaped vegetable that is related to a pumpkin.
22. An evening meal.
23. _____ a pie in the oven.

DOWN

1. A large, round, orange vegetable
2. _____ the turkey with a knife.
3. Americans _____ Thanksgiving in the autumn.
4. Gather the crops.
6. Something that protects the crops. Hint: It ends with W.

7. Families _____ together on Thanksgiving.
8. The ship that pilgrims came to America on.
9. A long journey over the ocean.
10. A sauce that is poured over turkey.
16. Something cooked inside the turkey and served at dinner.

17. The people on board the Mayflower.
19. The nut of an oak tree.
20. _____ the table before dinner.
21. Have a _____ of pumpkin pie for dessert.

🎁 Holidays and Celebrations

ACROSS

3. Valentine's Day activity: See a _____ at the theater.

5. Something people give their sweethearts on Valentine's Day.

6. Touch lips with someone.

8. Move your body to music.

9. The symbol of love.

11. A person who adores you without letting you know who he or she is: A _____ admirer.

14. The day on which Valentine's Day is celebrated.

15. A Valentine's Day emotion.

16. Something people give their sweethearts on Valentine's Day.

17. A Valentine's Day color.

18. Something people give their sweethearts on Valentine's Day.

20. Fall in love as soon as you see someone: Love at first _____.

21. Valentine's Day activity: Go on a _____.

23. Wrap your arms around someone.

24. The month in which Valentine's Day is celebrated.

DOWN

1. Words in a Valentine's Day card: Be _____.

2. Ask someone to marry you.

4. Part of a Valentine's Day rhyme: _____ are blue.

5. _____ in love.

7. Another way to say darling or honey.

10. Hug or kiss someone: Show _____.

12. A romantic date: A _____ dinner.

13. Something you send to your valentine.

17. Part of a Valentine's Day rhyme: _____ are red.

18. Secretly admire someone: Have a _____ on someone.

19. A cherub who makes people fall in love by shooting them with arrows.

20. Part of a Valentine's Day rhyme: _____ is sweet.

22. What cupid shoots you with.

104 New Year's Day

2. New Year's Eve activity: Go to a _____ .

3. New Year's resolution: Go on a _____ .

5. The last month of the year.

6. New Year's Eve activity: _____ "Auld Lang Syne."

8. A time when people rest from work or school and celebrate.

10. New Year's resolution: _____ weight.

12. New Year's Eve activity: Make a lot of _____ at midnight.

14. In with the _____ .

16. A promise made on New Year's Day.

19. New Year's resolution: _____ regularly.

21. The time of night when one day changes to the next.

23. New Year's resolution: Try _____ in school.

24. The final seconds before midnight on New Year's Eve.

DOWN

1. New Year's resolution: Be a _____ person.

3. New Year's Eve activity: _____ up in your best clothes.

4. People _____ New Year's on January first.

7. Something you change on New Year's Day. Hint: It lists the month of the year.

8. New Year's Day greeting: _____ New Year.

9. Tiny bits of paper thrown in the air at midnight.

11. Out with the _____ .

13. A time to ring in the New Year: At the _____ of midnight.

15. New Year's Eve activity: Get _____ with family and friends.

17. A time for parties: New Year's _____ .

18. The first month of the year.

20. New Year's resolution: _____ smoking.

22. New Year's resolution: Cut _____ on eating junk food.

Holidays and Celebrations

ACROSS

2. What British soldiers were called because of the color of their uniforms.

3. The location of the Tea Party.

6. A document that began the Revolutionary War: The _____ of Independence.

8. The season of Independence Day.

11. A document that outlines the basic rights and responsibilities of the government.

12. A nation's song: The national _____ .

14. American national anthem: "The Star-Spangled _____ ."

16. Another word for freedom.

21. Bright flashes in the sky seen on Independence Day.

22. The day of the month when Independence Day is celebrated.

24. A type of democracy led by a president who was elected by the people.

DOWN

1. A colonist who supported the British monarchy.

2. A time when citizens are overthrowing their government.

4. The national flag of the United States: The _____ and Stripes.

5. A colonist who fought against the British monarchy.

6. A system of government in which the people elect their rulers.

7. An area that is under the political control of another country.

9. A type of government led by a king.

10. Colors of the American flag: Red, white, and _____ .

13. A time when people take a break from work and celebrate.

15. The month when Independence Day is celebrated.

17. Money paid to the government.

18. The right to make your own decisions and do what you want.

19. The number of colonies at the time of independence.

20. An outdoor event in which people grill food.

23. A symbol of independence: The Liberty _____ in Philadelphia.

106 Veterans Day

2. Another word for protect.
6. The army, navy, and air force: The _____ forces.
8. The day of Veterans Day.
10. Another way to say "injured in battle."
12. A person who has fought in a war.
13. Think about something that has happened.
14. The branch of the military that defends a country's seas.
17. Another word for truce.
18. Another word for bravery.
19. A building or statue that was built to honor veterans.
21. Veterans Day honors those who have _____ in the military.
22. A flower people wear in memory of those who served.
24. A moment of _____ to remember those who gave their lives.
25. A conflict between countries.
26. Another word for fighting. Hint: It begins with C.

DOWN

1. The branch of the military that defends a country's land.
3. Another word for protect.
4. A time when two armies fight.
5. A person who is in the army.
7. A place where people are buried.
9. To give up something for other people.
11. The things a soldier must do: His or her _____.
14. The month of Veterans Day.
15. What a soldier wears.
16. A person who was killed or wounded in battle.
17. The branch of the military that defends a country's skies. (3,5)
20. Great courage during battle.
23. A time when there is no fighting.

🎁 Holidays and Celebrations

ACROSS

1. Icy spears that hang from your roof.
4. Santa's toy makers.
6. Three _____ men.
10. A place where elves make toys.
11. A song people sing at Christmas.
12. A common decoration for the top of the tree.
14. A bed for the baby Jesus.
17. Another word for bad.
19. The man in the red suit.
21. A common decoration for the top of the tree.
23. Ice that covers windows.
25. Something that is put on a Christmas tree to make it pretty.
26. A person who takes care of sheep.
28. A decoration you can ring.
29. A Christmas greeting: _____ Christmas!
31. A green leaf seen at Christmas.
32. A striped Christmas treat. (5,4)

DOWN

2. Bright things that people put on their roofs or around Christmas trees.
3. A thing that kids make when it snows.
5. Something that is hung by the fireplace.
7. The stingy old miser from *A Christmas Carol*.
8. Santa comes down the _____.
9. The month when Christmas is celebrated.
13. Another word for gift.
15. Something used to make cookies and houses.
16. Something that naughty children get for Christmas.
17. The place where Santa's workshop is located. (5,4)
18. Santa's laugh. (2,2,2)
20. The city where Jesus was born.
21. Santa's transportation.
22. Something you write to Santa.
24. A piece of snow.
27. Happy like Santa Claus.
30. The color of Santa's suit.

2. Eggs are usually hard _____ before they are decorated.

3. The season of Easter.

5. A baby sheep.

7. The opposite of lose.

10. A watery color used to decorate eggs.

11. An edible material that some bunnies are made from.

13. A baby bird.

14. Families get _____ on Easter.

20. Put something where no one can see it.

21. An Easter greeting: _____ Easter.

22. The month in which Easter is usually held.

23. Another word for rabbit.

DOWN

1. Having many colors.

4. The day of the week on which Easter is celebrated.

6. A month when Easter is sometimes held.

8. An Easter flower.

9. Something to hold your Easter eggs.

10. Children _____ eggs with pretty colors and patterns.

12. Children go on an Easter egg _____ to find hidden eggs.

15. Something people decorate on Easter.

16. A time when people rest from work or school and celebrate.

17. Jump like a rabbit.

18. The hard outer part of an egg.

19. An animal with long ears.

🎁 **Holidays and Celebrations**

ACROSS

2. St. Patrick was sold into _____ by pirates.

3. People who come from Ireland.

5. A celebration in which groups of people wearing costumes or playing in bands march down the street for spectators to see.

6. A holy person.

8. St. Patrick was _____ by pirates.

9. The color of St. Patrick's Day.

10. St. Patrick is the _____ saint of Ireland.

12. A person who makes shoes. Hint: It begins with C.

15. A mischievous fairy from Ireland.

17. A word (used to describe leprechauns) that means "likes to cause trouble."

18. Another name for Ireland: The _____ Isle.

DOWN

1. People _____ green for luck on St. Patrick's Day.

2. Another word for clover.

3. The country in which St. Patrick worked his miracles.

4. According to legend, St. Patrick got rid of all the _____ in Ireland.

5. A container for leprechaun gold.

7. The day on which St. Patrick's Day is celebrated.

9. A valuable, yellow metal.

11. Touch the _____ Stone for good luck.

13. An Irish spirit that wails loudly when someone is about to die.

14. An old story. Hint: It begins with L.

15. Good fortune.

16. Find a four-leaf _____ for good luck.

17. The month in which St. Patrick's Day is celebrated.

1. Buy environmentally _____ products.

7. Cut down on using _____ fuels.

8. Things we use that come from the earth: _____ resources.

9. _____ endangered species.

11. Resources that come back after we use them, such as wind or forests: _____ resources.

15. _____ a bike instead of driving a car.

16. Nature and everything in it.

18. A species with few animals remaining: An _____ species.

20. A layer of gas that protects us from UV rays: _____ layer.

22. Another word for garbage.

24. _____ a plastic bag when you go shopping instead of asking for a new one.

25. The place where trash ends up if it isn't recycled.

DOWN

1. _____ a leaky faucet.

2. A community of living things and their environment.

3. Development that doesn't destroy the environment: _____ development.

4. _____ a tree.

5. Use a resource wisely without wasting or destroying it.

6. _____ a sweater instead of using heat.

9. Chemicals and other garbage that harm nature.

10. Changing weather patterns due to global warming: _____ change.

12. _____ gases trap heat in Earth's atmosphere.

13. The increase of the average temperature of Earth due to the greenhouse effect: _____ warming.

14. Throw garbage on the ground.

15. _____ glass, cans, and newspaper.

17. Use less of something.

19. The planet we live on.

21. The month in which Earth Day is celebrated.

23. Harmful rain caused by pollution: _____ rain.

Crossword Puzzles by Type

 Word Skills   1, 7, 11, 19, 27, 35, 43, 51, 59, 67, 75, 83, 87, 90, 91, 94, 95, 96, 97

 All on a Theme   2, 4, 6, 8, 10, 12, 14, 16, 18, 20, 22, 24, 26, 28, 30, 32, 34, 36, 38, 40, 42, 44, 46, 48, 50, 52, 54, 56, 58, 60, 62, 64, 66, 68, 70, 72, 74, 76, 78, 80, 82, 84, 86, 88, 92, 100

 It's All Relative   3, 9, 17, 29, 37, 45, 53, 61, 69, 77, 85

 Collocation Awareness   5, 13, 21, 25, 33, 41, 49, 57, 65, 73, 81, 93, 99

 Fixed Phrases   15, 23, 31, 39, 47, 55, 63, 71, 79, 89, 98

 Holidays and Celebrations   101, 102, 103, 104, 105, 106, 107, 108, 109, 110

Answer Key

1. Opposite Adjectives

ACROSS: 1. Worst **5.** Kind **7.** Calm **8.** White **10.** Dry **11.** Fake **13.** Generous **18.** Raw **19.** Heavy **21.** Light **22.** Mild **23.** Bright **26.** Few **28.** Lazy **31.** Loose **32.** Last **33.** Hard **34.** Hot **35.** Happy

DOWN: 2. Rude **3.** False **4.** Poor **6.** New **7.** Common **9.** Thin **10.** Different **12.** Rough **14.** Early **15.** Straight **16.** Valuable **17.** Shallow **20.** Dirty **22.** Messy **24.** Healthy **25.** Short **26.** Fresh **27.** Wild **29.** Arid **30.** Near

2. The Weather

ACROSS: 1. Chilly **3.** Snow **4.** Lightning **9.** Hail **12.** Damp **13.** Cloudy **14.** Breeze **16.** Drizzle **18.** Snowman **21.** Fog **22.** Storm **23.** Rain **24.** Clear **25.** Tornado **26.** Precipitation

DOWN: 1. Calm **2.** Windy **3.** Sunshine **5.** Hurricane **6.** Cold **7.** Thunder **8.** Flood **10.** Umbrella **11.** Dry **14.** Blizzard **15.** Drought **17.** Zero **18.** Snowflake **19.** Shower **20.** Raindrop **21.** Forecast

3. Places in a City

ACROSS: 3. Hospital **5.** Museum **7.** Theater **9.** School **10.** Aquarium **12.** Pet **13.** Park **14.** Station **15.** Restaurant **17.** Gym **18.** Stop **20.** Prison **21.** Lot **22.** Department **23.** Bakery **25.** Highway **26.** Apartment

DOWN: 1. Cafe **2.** Sidewalk **4.** Intersection **6.** Mall **8.** Post **11.** University **12.** Playground **14.** Stadium **16.** Airport **19.** Gallery **21.** Library **22.** Dock **23.** Bank **24.** Road **25.** Home

4. On a Calendar

ACROSS: 1. Thursday **3.** Monday **5.** Third **9.** October **10.** June **11.** April **12.** December **14.** Friday **15.** Saturday **18.** Winter **20.** September **23.** Seven **24.** Weekend **25.** Second **26.** August **27.** Holiday

DOWN: 2. Spring **3.** March **4.** Sunday **6.** November **7.** Wednesday **8.** February **10.** July **13.** January **15.** Summer **16.** Autumn **17.** First **19.** Twelve **21.** May **22.** Tuesday

5. Reasons to Do Something 1

ACROSS: 1. Bakery **2.** Job **4.** Gym **6.** Muscles **7.** Helmet **11.** Alarm **13.** ATM **14.** Lotion **15.** Wallet **17.** Key **18.** Scale **19.** Socks **22.** Fire department **27.** Worm **28.** Diet **29.** Travel agent **30.** Red

DOWN: 1. Bike **3.** Blue **5.** Museum **7.** Hand **8.** E-mail **9.** Gloves **10.** Bank account **12.** Microscope **15.** Window **16.** Telescope **18.** Sweater **20.** Soap **21.** Door **22.** Folder **23.** Towel **24.** Number **25.** Cloth **26.** Fire

6. Colors, Numbers, Shapes

ACROSS: 2. Pink **3**. One **4**. White **6**. Six **7**. Blue **9**. Zero **10**. Rectangle **13**. Circle **14**. Green **16**. Orange **17**. Twelve **18**. Five **19**. Two **20**. Nine **21**. Seven **22**. Red

DOWN: 1. Yellow **2**. Purple **5**. Triangle **6**. Square **7**. Black **8**. Brown **11**. Three **12**. Eight **15**. Eleven **16**. Oval **18**. Four **19**. Ten

7. Irregular Plurals

ACROSS: 2. Fungi **4**. Teeth **5**. Feet **6**. Flies **8**. Zeroes **11**. Wishes **12**. People **15**. Elves **17**. Tomatoes **18**. Taxes **19**. Buses **22**. Berries **24**. Echoes **26**. Witches **28**. Spies **29**. Children

DOWN: 1. Leaves **3**. Geese **4**. Those **6**. Foxes **7**. Dishes **9**. Replies **10**. Dresses **11**. Women **13**. Potatoes **14**. Heroes **16**. Stories **19**. Benches **20**. Mice **21**. These **23**. Loaves **25**. Cacti **27**. Men

8. In a House

ACROSS: 1. Ceiling **3**. Bedroom **7**. Roof **10**. Dryer **11**. Stove **14**. Lamp **15**. Shelf **18**. Kitchen **19**. Bed **20**. Desk **21**. Toilet **25**. Cupboard **28**. Sofa **30**. TV **31**. Oven **32**. Picture **33**. Garage

DOWN: 1. Curtains **2**. Garden **4**. Door **5**. Mirror **6**. Closet **8**. Fireplace **9**. Basement **12**. Stairs **13**. Clock **16**. Fridge **17**. Window **19**. Bathroom **22**. Table **23**. Chair **24**. Counter **25**. Carpet **26**. Dining **27**. Freezer **29**. Yard

9. Jobs

ACROSS: 3. Plumber **5**. Fashion **6**. Hairdresser **10**. Architect **12**. Carrier **14**. Electrician **16**. Scientist **21**. Dentist **23**. Guide **24**. Chef **26**. Driver **27**. Agent

DOWN: 1. Mechanic **2**. Athlete **3**. Programmer **4**. Construction **5**. Firefighter **7**. Reporter **8**. Officer **9**. Farmer **11**. Teacher **13**. Actor **15**. Artist **16**. Singer **17**. Flight **18**. Janitor **19**. Baker **20**. Doctor **22**. Nurse **25**. Vet

10. Spring

ACROSS: 1. Flowers **7**. April **8**. Nest **10**. Sprout **11**. Shower **12**. Hibernation **14**. Eggs **15**. Melts **18**. Caterpillar **22**. May **23**. Daffodil **24**. Birds **26**. Hatch **28**. Tadpole **30**. Patrick's **32**. Roots **34**. Calf

DOWN: 1. Fools' **2**. March **3**. Garden **4**. Blossoms **5**. Earth **6**. Mother's Day **9**. Stem **13**. Tulip **16**. Farmer **17**. Lay **19**. Robin **20**. Lamb **21**. Plant **25**. Seeds **27**. Chick **29**. Plow **31**. Soil **33**. Thaw

11. Name the Category 1

ACROSS: 4. Shape **5**. Furniture **6**. Number **8**. Meat **10**. Flower **13**. Sport **14**. Insect **15**. Musician **17**. Mountain **18**. Game **20**. Artist **21**. Country **22**. Tool **24**. Nut **26**. Tree **27**. Bird **28**. Organ **29**. Vegetable

DOWN: 1. Fruit **2**. Month **3**. City **4**. Sense **7**. Ruler **8**. Media **9**. Continent **11**. River **12**. Reptile **13**. Scientist **15**. Mammal **16**. Berry **19**. Monster **23**. Ocean **24**. Noble **25**. Spice

12. Summer

ACROSS: 4. Park **5**. Tan **6**. Shorts **8**. Swimming **10**. Shells **11**. Tide **12**. Backyard **13**. Sunglasses **17**. Wave **18**. Vacation **22**. Sandcastle **23**. Barbecue **25**. Off **26**. Turn **27**. Camping **28**. Hike **29**. Keep

DOWN: 1. Fan **2**. Picnic **3**. Bikini **4**. Pool **5**. T-shirt **7**. Towel **8**. Sandals **9**. Weeds **10**. Shade **14**. Grass **15**. Sunscreen **16**. Swimsuit **19**. Barefoot **20**. Lemonade **21**. Cubes **24**. Beach

13. Chores

ACROSS: 2. Put **5**. Lock **7**. Weed **9**. Hang **11**. Run **12**. Iron **13**. Check **16**. Open **17**. Sweep **19**. Wash **21**. Water **23**. Vacuum **24**. Make **25**. Do **26**. Take

DOWN: 1. Set **2**. Pick **3**. Rake **4**. Fold **6**. Clean **8**. Turn **10**. Give **13**. Chop **14**. Mow **15**. Recycle **17**. Shovel **18**. Sort **20**. Dust **21**. Wipe **22**. Tidy

14. Autumn

ACROSS: 1. Leaf **3**. Corn **4**. Pick **6**. Salmon **8**. Ripe **9**. Pear **13**. Geese **14**. Crow **17**. Halloween **19**. Hay **20**. Chestnut **23**. Acorn **24**. November **28**. Maple **29**. Treat **30**. Crops **31**. Red **32**. Sunflower **34**. Rake

DOWN: 2. Foliage **3**. Chop **5**. Carve **6**. September **7**. Yellow **10**. Turkey **11**. Scarecrow **12**. Fall **15**. Gather **16**. Costume **18**. Autumn **21**. Bake **22**. Leaves **25**. October **26**. Brown **27**. Apple **29**. Turn **33**. Oak

15. Proverbs 1

ACROSS: 2. Lunch **4**. Preach **7**. Dog **9**. Leopard **10**. Skin **13**. Hands **14**. Variety **15**. Cart **16**. Go **17**. Absence **21**. Pot **22**. Feather **25**. Opportunity **28**. Merrier **29**. Poison **31**. Sight **32**. Evil **33**. Dogs **34**. Bite

DOWN: 1. Tools **2**. Leap **3**. Hay **5**. Eggs **6**. Practice **7**. Day **8**. Hindsight **11**. Prevention **12**. Wait **13**. Heat **18**. Cheap **19**. Revenge **20**. Boat **21**. Picture **23**. Ears **24**. Deserves **26**. Rains **27**. Wheel **28**. Might **29**. Pain **30**. Safe

16. Winter

ACROSS: 1. Ski **3**. Frost **5**. Minus **7**. Sweater **8**. Icicle **9**. Fire **11**. Drops **13**. February **14**. Hockey **16**. Angel **18**. Earmuffs **20**. Have **22**. Chocolate **23**. Celebrate **25**. Zero **28**. Resolution **29**. Sled

DOWN: 1. Scarf **2**. December **4**. Skate **5**. Make **6**. Slippery **7**. Snowflake **10**. Coat **12**. Boots **15**. Gloves **17**. Freeze **19**. Snowboard **20**. Hibernate **21**. Blizzard **23**. Covers **24**. Throw **26**. Cold **27**. Ice

17. Animal Descriptions

ACROSS: 1. Snail **2**. Chicken **4**. Deer **6**. Monkey **8**. Cat **9**. Bee **10**. Shark **14**. Penguin **15**. Giraffe **17**. Pig **18**. Scorpion **20**. Dog **22**. Mosquito **23**. Zebra **25**. Crocodile **26**. Rabbit **28**. Lion **29**. Turtle **30**. Dragonfly **32**. Wolf

DOWN: 1. Snake **2**. Cow **3**. Camel **4**. Duck **5**. Oyster **7**. Kangaroo **9**. Bear **11**. Elephant **12**. Tiger **13**. Sheep **16**. Fox **18**. Spider **19**. Squirrel **21**. Gorilla **24**. Bat **27**. Ant **31**. Owl

18. At a Restaurant

ACROSS: 1. Would **2.** Bowl **5.** Steak **7.** Salad **8.** Treat **11.** On **12.** Buffet **13.** Chopsticks **15.** Spoon **20.** Here **21.** Reservation **22.** Chinese **24.** Take **25.** Appetizer **27.** Spaghetti **29.** Plate **30.** Cup

DOWN: 1. Wait **2.** Bill **3.** Japanese **4.** Fast food **6.** Grab **9.** Fork **10.** Knife **14.** Order **15.** Sushi **16.** Dessert **17.** Menu **18.** Mexican **19.** Waiter **22.** Chef **23.** Pizza **26.** Pasta **28.** Tip

19. Category Plus Letter 1

ACROSS: 1. Goat **4.** May **5.** Circle **6.** Table **7.** Pacific **8.** Thumb **10.** Apple **13.** Europe **15.** Lungs **17.** Fox **22.** Shovel **23.** Train **25.** Grasshopper **28.** Pine **29.** Chair **31.** Winter **32.** Oak **33.** Carrot **35.** Tulip

DOWN: 2. Asia **3.** Lettuce **4.** Milk **5.** Coffee **7.** Peanut **9.** Beef **11.** Pig **12.** Six **14.** Octopus **16.** Spring **18.** Owl **19.** Yellow **20.** Math **21.** Tea **22.** Square **24.** Iron **26.** Parrot **27.** Crow **28.** Pink **30.** April **34.** Ant

20. At the Movies

ACROSS: 1. Popcorn **8.** Cinema **10.** Actor **11.** Director **12.** Theater **15.** Setting **16.** Synopsis **18.** Character **20.** Credits **21.** Climax **24.** Science fiction **27.** Romance **28.** Sequel **29.** Play **30.** Role

DOWN: 2. Plot **3.** Critic **4.** Scene **5.** Horror **6.** Fantasy **7.** Genre **9.** Action **13.** Star **14.** Soundtrack **16.** Special **17.** Subtitles **19.** Animation **22.** About **23.** Costume **25.** Comedy **26.** Film

21. Word Association 1

ACROSS: 1. Eggs **4.** Sugar **6.** Foe **7.** Alive **8.** Conclusion **10.** Coast **11.** Longitude **12.** Stones **15.** Take **16.** Gatherer **18.** Paper **20.** Arrow **21.** Place **22.** Dawn **26.** Fork **28.** End **29.** Tails **30.** Day **31.** Worse

DOWN: 1. Effect **2.** Balances **3.** Nail **4.** Sunset **5.** Treat **9.** Cons **11.** Last **13.** Toe **14.** Earth **16.** Grave **17.** Thread **18.** Prey **19.** Pepper **23.** White **24.** Dad **25.** Pole **27.** Key

22. Food and Cooking

ACROSS: 1. Burn **4.** Pork **6.** Spicy **7.** Soup **9.** Heat **10.** Fruit **11.** Seafood **13.** Fry **15.** Snack **17.** Dinner **18.** Dessert **21.** Corn **22.** Beef **26.** Vegetables **27.** Slice **29.** Lunch **30.** Raw **31.** Salad **32.** Bake **33.** Oven **34.** Sweet **35.** Boil **36.** Poultry

DOWN: 2. Rice **3.** Fish **4.** Pasta **5.** Sour **6.** Spices **8.** Pour **11.** Stale **12.** Dairy **13.** Freezer **14.** Mild **16.** Kitchen **19.** Stove **20.** Breakfast **23.** Fresh **24.** Salt **25.** Well done **28.** Cereal **34.** Stir

23. Similes 1

ACROSS: 1. Cold **3.** Laugh **8.** Dead **9.** Green **10.** Grin **11.** Black **12.** Peas **16.** Sly **18.** Easy **20.** White **24.** Stand out **25.** Pretty **26.** Sick **27.** Out **28.** Silent **30.** Read **32.** Light **33.** Drop **34.** Cry

DOWN: 2. Leak **4.** Avoid **5.** Hard **6.** Feel **7.** Sink **8.** Deep **11.** Busy **13.** Slow **14.** Sleep **15.** Slippery **17.** Stubborn **19.** Spread **21.** Old **22.** Flat **23.** Quick **24.** Smooth **26.** Sharp **29.** Eat **31.** Dry

24. Fruits and Vegetables

ACROSS: 3. Spinach **6**. Peach **7**. Melon **9**. Cabbage **11**. Apple **13**. Tomato **14**. Peas **16**. Broccoli **18**. Carrot **19**. Pineapple **21**. Corn **23**. Grapes **26**. Blueberry **28**. Pumpkin **29**. Mushroom

DOWN: 1. Strawberry **2**. Cauliflower **4**. Wheat **5**. Celery **8**. Lemon **9**. Cherry **10**. Beans **12**. Potato **15**. Onion **16**. Banana **17**. Orange **18**. Cucumber **20**. Lettuce **22**. Rice **23**. Garlic **24**. Pear **25**. Squash **27**. Plum

25. Before, During, After

ACROSS: 2. Pick **4**. Cheer **5**. Put **7**. Open **9**. Ask **10**. Clap **12**. Knock **14**. Get **16**. See **18**. Blow **20**. Eat **22**. Listen **23**. Wear **25**. Stomp **27**. Brush **28**. Order **29**. Purchase **32**. Set **33**. Pay **34**. Find

DOWN: 1. Drink **3**. Clean **4**. Check **6**. Tip **8**. Make **10**. Call **11**. Answer **13**. Build **15**. Take **17**. Wash **18**. Borrow **19**. Celebrate **21**. Try **24**. Turn **25**. Shrug **26**. Wipe **30**. Hand **31**. Study **32**. Say

26. Travel

ACROSS: 4. One-way **6**. Port **8**. Luggage **9**. Station **10**. Holiday **11**. Beach **13**. Train **14**. Suitcase **17**. Round **18**. Pack **19**. Service **20**. Agent **22**. Resort **26**. Bag **27**. Airport **29**. Show **30**. Passport

DOWN: 1. Pool **2**. Vacation **3**. Cruise **5**. Visa **7**. Departure **11**. Backpack **12**. Check **13**. Tent **14**. Souvenir **15**. Hotel **16**. Gift **20**. Arrival **21**. Honeymoon **23**. Ship **24**. Tourist **25**. Ferry **26**. Book **28**. Trip

27. Irregular Past Tense

ACROSS: 2. Fell **4**. Saw **8**. Shot **9**. Shook **10**. Made **12**. Began **14**. Wrote **16**. Threw **17**. Did **21**. Gave **22**. Woke **23**. Wore **25**. Caught **27**. Drank **29**. Hid **30**. Slept **33**. Grew **36**. Found **37**. Told **38**. Bit

DOWN: 1. Chose **3**. Lost **4**. Spoke **5**. Swam **6**. Meant **7**. Fought **11**. Drove **12**. Blew **13**. Got **14**. Won **15**. Brought **17**. Drew **18**. Stole **19**. Became **20**. Bought **24**. Ran **26**. Had **27**. Dug **28**. Ate **31**. Left **32**. Met **34**. Rode **35**. Went

28. Health and Sickness

ACROSS: 3. Black eye **6**. Well **8**. Cavity **9**. Rest **11**. Run **12**. Shape **15**. Surgery **17**. Nurse **18**. Sprained **19**. Pharmacy **25**. Patient **26**. Cut **28**. Optometrist **29**. Ill **30**. Scratch **31**. Feet

DOWN: 1. Medicine **2**. Fever **3**. Bruise **4**. Cough **5**. Allergy **7**. Down **9**. Rash **10**. Sore **13**. Prescription **14**. Headache **16**. Runny **18**. Symptom **20**. Hospital **21**. Dentist **22**. Flu **23**. Doctor **24**. Clinic **26**. Catch **27**. Take **30**. See

29. Tool Descriptions

ACROSS: 2. Saw **3**. Brush **8**. Filter **9**. Compass **11**. Door **12**. Pen **14**. String **16**. Pot **18**. Spoon **20**. Telescope **24**. Axe **26**. Plow **27**. Lamp **28**. Eraser **29**. Internet **33**. Wallet **34**. Fork **35**. Rake

DOWN: 1. Knife **2**. Scissors **3**. Broom **4**. Belt **5**. Fence **6**. Microscope **7**. Hose **10**. Ship **13**. Needle **15**. Glue **17**. Telephone **18**. Shovel **19**. Net **21**. Staple **22**. Chopsticks **23**. Tape **25**. Thread **26**. Pan **30**. Towel **31**. Ruler **32**. Hook

30. Sports

ACROSS: 1. Block **4.** Judge **7.** Coach
10. Quarter **11.** Racket **12.** Athlete
16. Trophy **18.** Stadium **20.** Soccer
24. Diamond **25.** Fan **26.** Goalkeeper
28. Opponent **31.** Tennis **32.** Serve

DOWN: 2. Court **3.** Beat **5.** Glove **6.** Score
8. Hockey **9.** Basketball **13.** Half
14. Equipment **15.** Whistle **17.** Record
19. Inning **21.** Champion **22.** Referee
23. Foul **27.** Bat **29.** Pass **30.** Tie

31. Idioms 1

ACROSS: 1. Time **3.** Point **5.** Weather **7.** Ways
10. Tied **11.** Recipe **12.** Air **13.** Red
15. Music **18.** Up **19.** Apart **20.** Brain
22. Shoulder **24.** Hand

DOWN: 1. Towel **2.** While **3.** Profile **4.** Thin
6. Eye **8.** Storm **9.** Overboard **12.** Arms
14. Doctor **16.** Second **17.** Course **20.** Boat
21. Add **23.** Leg

32. Clothing

ACROSS: 1. Tight **3.** Skirt **4.** Scarf **6.** Cotton
7. Coat **9.** Shoes **11.** Gloves **15.** Blouse
17. Belt **18.** Hat **19.** Jacket **20.** Try
21. Secondhand **23.** Silk **25.** Pajamas
26. Polka **27.** Trend **30.** Match **31.** Striped
32. Shorts

DOWN: 2. Good **3.** Sandals **5.** Fits **8.** Loose
9. Shirt **10.** Wool **12.** Fashion **13.** Boots
14. Sweater **15.** Baggy **16.** Socks **17.** Button
19. Jeans **22.** Dress **24.** Leather **25.** Pants
28. Suit **29.** Tie

33. Amounts, Groups, and Containers

ACROSS: 1. Jug **3.** Bunch **6.** Pair **7.** Swarm
8. Stack **9.** Pod **11.** Bowl **12.** Coil **14.** Clove
15. Box **17.** Deck **19.** Litter **21.** Herd
23. Spoonful **25.** Pile **26.** List **27.** Can
28. Loaf **29.** Cup **30.** Head

DOWN: 1. Jar **2.** Glass **3.** Bar **4.** Handful **5.** Pot
6. Pack **8.** Slice **9.** Pride **10.** Flock **11.** Bag
13. Bottle **15.** Ball **16.** School **17.** Drop
18. Fleet **20.** Tube **22.** Roll **23.** Sack **24.** Field
25. Piece

34. Transportation

ACROSS: 2. Bus **4.** Red **6.** Jam **8.** Fare
9. Car **11.** Sign **13.** Airplane **14.** Helmet
17. Ship **18.** Train **19.** Vehicle **21.** Rush
22. Alley **23.** Highway **24.** Truck **25.** Camel
28. Rocket **31.** Pedestrian **34.** Horse **35.** Lot
36. Subway

DOWN: 1. Crosswalk **2.** Bicycle **3.** Street
5. Bridge **7.** Mechanic **10.** Intersection
12. Garage **15.** Motorcycle **16.** Zone
20. Helicopter **26.** Belt **27.** Green **28.** Road
29. Tunnel **30.** Limit **32.** Ferry **33.** Gas

35. Synonyms 1

ACROSS: 2. Rich **5.** Attack **8.** Tug **9.** Talk
11. End **13.** Mistake **16.** Near **17.** Right
18. Come **19.** Evil **20.** Peak **21.** Enemy
24. Sick **25.** Laugh **26.** Smart **29.** Difficult
31. Sprint **32.** Push **33.** Little **35.** Want
36. Angry

DOWN: 1. Hurt **2.** Rock **3.** Hate **4.** Suggest
6. Chair **7.** Strange **10.** Location
12. Whisper **14.** Understand **15.** Lucky
17. Remember **22.** Easy **23.** Yell **24.** Shout
26. Start **27.** Answer **28.** Throw **30.** Fast
34. Try

36. Space

ACROSS: 2. Universe **4.** Moon **10.** Sun
11. Astronaut **12.** Earth **14.** Rotates
16. Constellation **17.** Mars **19.** Star
20. Revolve **21.** Galaxy **23.** Comet **26.** Black
27. Venus **29.** Jupiter **30.** Planet **31.** Phases

DOWN: 1. Nebula **3.** Rocket **5.** Neptune
6. Asteroid **7.** Shooting **8.** Telescope
9. Astronomer **13.** Milky **15.** Saturn
18. Shower **19.** Solar **21.** Gravity **22.** Orbit
23. Crater **24.** Eclipse **25.** Uranus **28.** Spots

37. Times When

ACROSS: 3. Summer **6.** October **7.** Afternoon
9. Dawn **12.** Autumn **14.** Drought
16. Harvest **17.** Rush **20.** Halloween
23. Eclipse **25.** Easter **26.** Valentine's
28. Noon **29.** April Fools' **30.** Night

DOWN: 1. Vacation **2.** December **4.** Morning
5. Flood **8.** New Year's **10.** Winter
11. January **13.** Spring **15.** Thanksgiving
18. Sale **19.** Christmas **21.** Election
22. Birthday **24.** Evening **27.** Dusk

38. School Verbs

ACROSS: 1. Form **3.** Put **6.** Figure **9.** Watch
10. Read **11.** Solve **12.** Contrast **13.** Do
14. Understand **18.** Eat **20.** Summarize
23. Describe **24.** Pass **26.** Play **27.** Ask
28. Sing **30.** Open

DOWN: 2. Raise **3.** Predict **4.** Tell **5.** Observe
7. Hand **8.** Fail **9.** Write **11.** Study
12. Compare **13.** Draw **15.** Recite
16. Demonstrate **17.** Answer **19.** Take
21. Mark **22.** Explain **25.** Make **29.** Go

39. Lexical Chunks

ACROSS: 4. Were **5.** Time **7.** Hand **8.** Think
11. Call **13.** View **15.** Like **16.** Order
17. Should **18.** Short **20.** Said **22.** You
25. Mind **27.** Kidding **28.** Trying **29.** Going

DOWN: 1. Put **2.** Been **3.** Believe **6.** Ask **7.** Hear
9. Ready **10.** Ever **12.** Later **14.** Words
17. Saying **18.** Speak **19.** Talking **21.** Don't
23. Up **24.** Bad **25.** Mean **26.** Far

40. Geography: On a Map

ACROSS: 2. Tropical **6.** Bay **7.** Peninsula
10. Pole **11.** Equator **12.** Town
13. Scale **15.** Plateau **16.** City **18.** River
19. Hemisphere **20.** Country **22.** Range
24. Lake **25.** Archipelago **27.** Village
28. Desert **29.** Latitude

DOWN: 1. Map **3.** Rose **4.** Polar **5.** Altitude
6. Border **8.** Island **9.** West **12.** Temperate
13. South **14.** Longitude **16.** Capital
17. Key **20.** Continent **21.** Ocean **23.** Globe
26. Coast

41. Verb Collocations 1

ACROSS: 1. Set **4.** Reach **7.** Follow **8.** Throw
10. Make **12.** Drop **14.** Burst **16.** Break
17. Say **18.** Speak **20.** Mind **21.** Draw
22. Pass **24.** Spread

DOWN: 2. Talk **3.** Shoot **5.** Commit **6.** Save
7. Find **9.** Hit **11.** Keep **13.** Place **14.** Buy
15. Stand **17.** Skip **19.** Play **20.** Miss **21.** Do
23. Cause **25.** Raise **26.** Get

42. Fitness and Health

ACROSS: 4. Sit **6.** Quit **9.** Gym **10.** Stamina **12.** Protein **14.** Work **16.** Hiking **22.** Skipping **23.** Out **24.** Down **27.** Minerals **29.** Calories **30.** Balanced **32.** Scale **33.** Check

DOWN: 1. Lift **2.** Yoga **3.** Jumping **5.** Trainer **7.** Swimming **8.** Blood **11.** Aerobics **13.** Push **15.** Shape **17.** Jogging **18.** Coordination **19.** Endurance **20.** Towel **21.** Stretch **25.** Athlete **26.** Heart **27.** Muscle **28.** Speed **30.** Bone **31.** Diet

43. Category Plus Rhymes

ACROSS: 2. Crowd **3.** Witch **4.** Table **5.** Fog **8.** Fork **10.** Jack **12.** Rice **13.** Ten **14.** Eight **17.** Paw **19.** Pear **21.** South **23.** Blue **24.** Deer **25.** East **27.** Rain **28.** Yellow **30.** May **32.** Ocean **35.** Stream

DOWN: 1. Head **2.** Chair **3.** West **6.** Green **7.** Corn **8.** Foot **9.** Kite **10.** June **11.** Knife **15.** Horse **16.** Flute **18.** Wheat **19.** Plum **20.** Cherry **22.** Shell **23.** Bear **24.** Drum **26.** Spoon **29.** Herd **31.** Arm **33.** Cow **34.** Ace

44. Fantasy

ACROSS: 3. Unicorn **6.** Curse **8.** Hero **10.** Grant **11.** Bandit **13.** Goblin **14.** Wish **15.** Legend **19.** Fairy **20.** Map **21.** Giant **22.** Witch **24.** Invisible **27.** Sorcerer **29.** Dragon **31.** Werewolf **33.** Spell **34.** Medusa **35.** Troll

DOWN: 1. Pirate **2.** Skeleton **4.** Cave **5.** Wizard **7.** Zombie **8.** Haunted **9.** Knight **12.** Dwarf **15.** Lamp **16.** Vampire **17.** Myth **18.** Under **23.** Castle **25.** Break **26.** Ogre **28.** Cyclops **29.** Desert **30.** Cast **32.** Wand

45. Things That People Do

ACROSS: 2. Letter **5.** Car **7.** Book **8.** Dishes **9.** Net **11.** Eye **12.** Shoulders **14.** Bed **15.** Hat **17.** Movie **19.** Hair **20.** Nest **24.** Sandcastle **27.** Web **29.** Horse **30.** Egg **32.** TV **33.** Airplane **34.** Fish **35.** Feet

DOWN: 1. Window **3.** Telephone **4.** Door **5.** Cake **6.** Game **7.** Ball **9.** Nose **10.** Teeth **13.** Umbrella **16.** Test **17.** Money **18.** Light **21.** Radio **22.** Helmet **23.** Flower **24.** Snowman **25.** Spoon **26.** Chair **28.** Bee **31.** Gift

46. Feelings

ACROSS: 2. Curious **5.** Jealous **8.** Tired **11.** Pessimistic **12.** Worried **13.** Envy **14.** Excited **16.** Afraid **17.** Thirsty **19.** Heart **21.** Frightened **23.** Hungry **25.** Embarrassed **27.** Cold **28.** Depressed

DOWN: 1. Fall **2.** Confused **3.** Optimistic **4.** Mad **6.** Surprised **7.** Anxious **9.** Confident **10.** Disappointed **15.** Chilly **18.** Angry **19.** Hot **20.** Annoyed **21.** Forward **22.** Express **24.** Proud **26.** Sad

47. Phrasal Verbs 1: Context Plus Collocation

ACROSS: 1. Go, **2.** Face, **4.** Throw, **6.** Lay, **7.** Sit, **8.** Put, **9.** Cross, **11.** Catch, **13.** Look, **14.** Set, **15.** Check, **17.** End, **19.** Run, **20.** Log, **21.** Do, **22.** Tell, **23.** Rip.

DOWN: 1. Get, **2.** Fall, **3.** Hit, **5.** Watch, **7.** Stop, **8.** Pick, **10.** Stick, **12.** Cut, **13.** Live, **14.** Stand, **16.** Call, **18.** Drop.

48. Science 1

ACROSS: 2. Magma **4**. Attract **7**. Refract **9**. Sound **10**. Heat **11**. Cycle **12**. Mass **15**. Gas **16**. Matter **19**. Microscope **21**. Paleontologist **24**. Reflect **26**. Measure **27**. Planet **28**. Velocity **31**. Fossil **32**. Solid **33**. Force **34**. Astronomer

DOWN: 1. Freeze **3**. Mathematician **5**. Condense **6**. DNA **8**. Axis **13**. Star **14**. Telescope **15**. Geologist **16**. Magnetism **17**. Evaporate **18**. Melt **20**. Extinct **22**. Theory **23**. Friction **25**. Classify **27**. Prove **29**. Pole **30**. Data

49. Job Verb Collocations

ACROSS: 3. Play **4**. Cook **6**. Act **7**. Bake **8**. Cut **12**. Clean **13**. Do **14**. Solve **15**. Design **17**. Write **18**. Grow **19**. Take **20**. Serve **21**. Raise **23**. Heal

DOWN: 1. Fly **2**. Book **3**. Put **5**. Catch **7**. Build **9**. Tell **10**. Make **11**. Sing **13**. Deliver **14**. Sew **15**. Drive **16**. Repair **18**. Give **19**. Teach **20**. Sell **22**. Draw

50. The Human Body

ACROSS: 1. Muscle **7**. Exhale **8**. Tendon **9**. Lungs **11**. Ligament **12**. Feet **14**. Digest **16**. Teeth **17**. Nervous **20**. Circulatory **24**. Elbow **26**. Brain **28**. Knee **30**. Hand **31**. Wrist

DOWN: 2. Cartilage **3**. Inhale **4**. Fingers **5**. Heart **6**. Digestive **10**. Skeletal **12**. Fat **13**. Toes **15**. Stomach **16**. Tongue **17**. Nerve **18**. Respiratory **19**. Nose **21**. Ribs **22**. Ankle **23**. Jaw **25**. Blood **26**. Bone **27**. Neck **29**. Eyes

51. Opposite Verbs

ACROSS: 2. Find **3**. Borrow **6**. Receive **9**. Close **10**. Hate **11**. Melt **12**. Stop **14**. Catch **16**. Lose **17**. Fill **19**. Deny **20**. Fix **21**. Combine **22**. Stand **24**. Shrink **26**. Play **28**. Exit **29**. Prohibit **30**. Die

DOWN: 1. Attack **2**. Follow **3**. Believe **4**. Run **5**. Whisper **6**. Remember **7**. Criticize **8**. Miss **13**. Pull **15**. Cry **18**. Pick up **19**. Destroy **20**. Fail **23**. Arrive **24**. Spend **25**. Raise **26**. Put on **27**. Answer

52. Crime and Punishment

ACROSS: 1. Vandalism **7**. Court **8**. Shoplift **9**. Smuggle **10**. Witness **13**. Fine **16**. Law **17**. Evidence **21**. Break **22**. Murder **23**. Victim **25**. Pickpocket **27**. Detective **28**. Bars **29**. DNA **31**. Innocent **32**. Judge

DOWN: 2. Accuse **3**. Suspect **4**. Trial **5**. Interrogate **6**. Police officer **11**. Sentence **12**. Blackmail **14**. Alibi **15**. Time **18**. Convicted **19**. Arrest **20**. Jury **24**. Charged **26**. Prison **30**. Away

53. Places Around the World

ACROSS: 1. New York **6**. Athens **7**. Mexico **9**. India **11**. Saudi Arabia **12**. North America **16**. Paris **19**. Australia **22**. Atlantic **24**. Egypt **26**. Africa **27**. Berlin **28**. Mecca

DOWN: 2. Russia **3**. China **4**. Pacific **5**. London **8**. Arctic **10**. Europe **13**. Antarctica **14**. Indian **15**. Asia **17**. South America **18**. Brazil **20**. Spain **21**. Japan **23**. Greece **25**. Peru

54. The Environment

ACROSS: 1. Bicycle **5**. Shower **7**. Extinct **8**. Lights **9**. Toxic **10**. Pollution **14**. Solar **16**. Disposable **18**. Acid **19**. Recycle **22**. Reuse **23**. Friendly **24**. Organic **26**. Climate **28**. Sweater **29**. Earth **30**. Greenhouse

DOWN: 2. Litter **3**. Brushing **4**. Warming **6**. Pesticide **11**. Landfill **12**. Garbage **13**. Loss **15**. Leaky **17**. Ozone **20**. Carbon **21**. Endangered **22**. Reduce **25**. Green **27**. Trash

55. Things People Say

ACROSS: 1. Trespassing **4**. Find **5**. Seated **7**. Anything **8**. Receipt **12**. Here **13**. Ticket **16**. Exit **17**. Seat belts **19**. Deposit **21**. Tax **22**. Rest **23**. Help **25**. Open **27**. Feed **28**. Fluids **29**. Hurt **30**. Slippery

DOWN: 2. Ready **3**. Shoplifters **4**. Fishing **5**. Show **6**. Particular **9**. Check **10**. Due **11**. Case **14**. Take **15**. License **18**. Total **20**. Take-off **24**. Popcorn **25**. Order **26**. Fill

56. At School

ACROSS: 1. Correct **3**. Bus **5**. Class **7**. Math **8**. Due **9**. History **10**. Take **14**. Student **16**. Principal **17**. Notes **19**. Out **20**. Desk **22**. Blackboard **24**. Art **25**. Ask **26**. Graph **31**. Music **33**. Science **34**. Solve **35**. Raise

DOWN: 2. Teacher **3**. Bully **4**. Understand **6**. Social **7**. Measure **11**. Map **12**. Mistake **13**. Scissors **15**. Textbook **16**. Pen **18**. Mark **21**. Eraser **23**. Assignment **27**. Answer **28**. Cause **29**. Pupil **30**. Field **32**. Pass

57. Verb Collocations 2

ACROSS: 1. Shoot **3**. Fail **5**. Go **6**. Talk **7**. Set **8**. Keep **10**. Draw **12**. Buy **13**. Play **14**. Pass **16**. Take **17**. Save **18**. Spread **21**. Commit **23**. Place **24**. Wash **26**. Cause **27**. See

DOWN: 1. Stand **2**. Tell **3**. Face **4**. Look **5**. Give **7**. Say **9**. Pay **11**. Waste **12**. Burst **13**. Put **15**. Catch **17**. Skip **19**. Fix **20**. Reach **22**. Miss **25**. Speak

58. Math

ACROSS: 1. Angle **3**. Decimal **5**. Divide **7**. Triangle **9**. Perimeter **11**. Obtuse **12**. Odd **13**. Radius **14**. Estimate **19**. Volume **20**. Point **21**. Circumference **22**. Area **24**. Parallel **26**. Fraction **27**. Width **28**. Height

DOWN: 1. Add **2**. Cube **3**. Degrees **4**. Negative **6**. Infinite **8**. Denominator **9**. Perpendicular **10**. Root **15**. Sphere **16**. Maximum **17**. Average **18**. Even **20**. Percent **23**. Acute **24**. Prime **25**. Length

59. Irregular Past Participles

ACROSS: 1. Risen **3**. Bitten **5**. Brought **8**. Rung **11**. Driven **13**. Eaten **14**. Swum **16**. Shone **17**. Burnt **18**. Felt **19**. Chosen **21**. Struck **22**. Grown **24**. Spoken **25**. Forbidden **27**. Told **29**. Blown **30**. Known **31**. Sung **32**. Worn

DOWN: 2. Seen **4**. Torn **6**. Gone **7**. Thrown **8**. Ridden **9**. Given **10**. Done **12**. Been **15**. Mistaken **16**. Stung **18**. Forgotten **20**. Found **23**. Shrunk **24**. Sunk **25**. Flown **26**. Drunk **28**. Drawn

60. Wonders of Nature

ACROSS: 4. Soil **7.** Leaves **9.** Ocean **10.** Hill **11.** Wave **12.** Cave **13.** Desert **14.** Tide **15.** Dew **20.** Tundra **21.** Plateau **22.** Iceberg **23.** Stars **24.** Rainforest **27.** Moon **29.** Alpine **31.** Stream **32.** Savanna **33.** Rainbow **34.** Valley

DOWN: 1. Frost **2.** Sun **3.** Lake **5.** Lightning **6.** Beach **8.** Shadow **11.** Wetland **16.** Mountain **17.** Glacier **18.** Prairie **19.** Waterfall **22.** Icicle **23.** Shore **25.** Reef **26.** Snowflake **28.** Volcano **30.** Peak

61. Parts and Pieces

ACROSS: 1. Gloves **5.** Finger **6.** Bed **7.** Ear **8.** Shorts **9.** Pedals **10.** Root **12.** Rudder **15.** Nose **17.** Image **18.** Deck **20.** Sail **21.** Text **23.** Leaf **26.** Link **27.** Necklace **30.** Sofa **31.** Handlebars

DOWN: 1. Geometry **2.** Air force **3.** Heart **4.** Flower **6.** Bracelet **8.** Seed **11.** Trunk **13.** Eye **14.** Gills **16.** Stem **19.** Chain **20.** Stomach **22.** Fin **23.** Lung **24.** Algebra **25.** Table **28.** Chair **29.** Army **30.** Socks

62. The Olympics

ACROSS: 1. High **5.** Volleyball **7.** Diving **10.** Athlete **12.** Four **13.** Gymnastics **18.** Nationality **20.** Medal **21.** Fencing **23.** Silver **24.** Long **27.** Record **28.** Referee **29.** Bronze

DOWN: 2. Gold **3.** Judge **4.** Cycling **6.** Anthem **8.** Vault **9.** Archery **11.** Torch **14.** Shot **15.** Swimming **16.** Rings **17.** Hurdles **19.** Track **20.** Marathon **22.** Goalkeeper **24.** Lap **25.** Podium **26.** Sprint **27.** Relay

63. Proverbs 2

ACROSS: 2. Chickens **8.** Leap **10.** Day **11.** Reap **12.** Horse **15.** Company **17.** Dogs **18.** Alike **20.** Ears **22.** Believing **23.** Evil **24.** Sight **26.** Haste **28.** Go **30.** Tools **32.** Rains **33.** Good **34.** Preach **35.** Fire **36.** Business **37.** Leopard

DOWN: 1. Kill **3.** Cheap **4.** End **5.** Fish **6.** Safety **7.** Err **9.** Practice **13.** Dog **14.** Boat **16.** Prevention **17.** Devil **19.** Lunch **21.** Silver **22.** Beggars **24.** Safe **25.** Eggs **27.** Action **29.** Might **31.** Succeed **34.** Pain

64. Relationships

ACROSS: 1. Hang **4.** Twin **8.** Acquaintance **9.** Ask **14.** Common **15.** Relative **16.** Keep **18.** Along **21.** Wife **22.** Out **23.** Single **24.** Boss **25.** Close **28.** Neighbor **30.** Groom **31.** Text **32.** Mentor

DOWN: 1. Husband **2.** Differences **3.** Teacher **5.** Break **6.** Sense **7.** Engagement **10.** Seeing **11.** Apart **12.** Bride **13.** Coworker **17.** Propose **19.** Argue **20.** Sibling **21.** Wedding **26.** Sight **27.** Good **29.** Hit

65. Adjective Noun Collocations

ACROSS: 1. Tender **4.** Sharp **7.** Fresh **9.** Strict **12.** Golden **15.** Necessary **18.** Minor **19.** Reasonable **22.** Dirty **24.** Background **25.** Good **26.** Fair

DOWN: 2. Nuclear **3.** Easy **5.** Antique **6.** Prompt **8.** Single **10.** Safe **11.** Close **13.** Casual **14.** Major **16.** Constructive **17.** Heavy **18.** Mild **20.** Ancient **21.** Square **22.** Deep **23.** Regular **26.** Fast

66. On the Job

ACROSS: 2. Retire **4**. Resume **7**. Quit **10**. Training **12**. Employee **14**. Fired **15**. Part **17**. Hire **18**. Contract **20**. Interview **21**. Rush **22**. Income **24**. Commute **26**. Skills **27**. Shift **28**. Strike **29**. Bonus

DOWN: 1. Form **2**. Resign **3**. Minimum **5**. Apply **6**. Net **7**. Qualifications **8**. Full **9**. Benefits **11**. Incentive **12**. Employer **13**. Experience **16**. Wage **17**. Help **19**. Boss **23**. Salary **25**. Union

67. Alliteration 1

ACROSS: 1. Trick **4**. Dawn **6**. Railroad **8**. Below **10**. Wild **12**. Helping **14**. Warm **15**. Tit **16**. Cut **18**. Fish **19**. Greenhouse **21**. Pretty **22**. Look **23**. Worrywart **26**. Hold **28**. Copycat **31**. Busy **32**. Ding **33**. Dime

DOWN: 2. Chocolate **3**. Zigzag **5**. Word **7**. Down **9**. Mountain **11**. Firefighter **12**. Hit **13**. Crash **16**. Creepy **17**. Blood **18**. Fossil **20**. Wicked **24**. Recycle **25**. Tick **27**. Love **28**. Candy **29**. Penny **30**. Turn.

68. Books and Stories

ACROSS: 1. Biography **3**. Set **6**. Science **7**. Plot **8**. Romance **9**. Dialogue **14**. Fiction **15**. Fantasy **17**. Novel **19**. Antagonist **20**. Comic **23**. Protagonist **24**. Illustrator **25**. Mystery

DOWN: 2. Past **4**. Title **5**. Hero **7**. Place **8**. Resolution **10**. Main **11**. Author **12**. Conflict **13**. Western **15**. Future **16**. Nonfiction **18**. Character **19**. Adventure **20**. Chapter **21**. Minor **22**. Climax **23**. Play

69. People Descriptions

ACROSS: 1. Casualty **3**. Criminal **5**. Model **6**. Patriot **7**. Detective **9**. Sailor **11**. Spy **12**. Inventor **15**. Historian **18**. Paleontologist **20**. Explorer **22**. Star **23**. Parent **24**. Nomad **25**. Refugee

DOWN: 1. Comedian **2**. Civilian **4**. Astronaut **6**. Pedestrian **8**. Citizen **10**. Witness **13**. Hostage **14**. Victim **16**. Teller **17**. Astronomer **19**. Orphan **21**. Pirate

70. Animal Kingdom

ACROSS: 1. Mammal **4**. Pack **6**. Bird **7**. Egg **9**. Insect **11**. Herd **12**. Tail **15**. Omnivore **16**. Fur **18**. Blubber **20**. Food chain **22**. Paws **23**. Hibernate **25**. Fangs **28**. Shell **31**. Habitat **32**. Gills **33**. Tusks

DOWN: 2. Marine **3**. Feathers **4**. Prey **5**. Carnivore **8**. Extinct **10**. Endangered **13**. Herbivore **14**. Nocturnal **16**. Food web **17**. Migrate **19**. Fish **21**. Claws **24**. Reptile **26**. Scales **27**. Wings **29**. Horns **30**. Lungs

71. Similes 2

ACROSS: 1. Sink **2**. Watch **4**. Out **6**. Feel **8**. Sly **10**. Black **11**. Cool **13**. Hard **15**. Sharp **16**. Easy **18**. Peas **20**. Avoid **22**. Blind **23**. Clean **24**. Old **26**. Different **28**. Dry **30**. Pretty **32**. Silent **33**. Good

DOWN: 1. Stubborn **3**. Cry **5**. Leak **6**. Flat **7**. Sick **8**. Smooth **9**. Sleep **12**. White **14**. Free **15**. Stand out **17**. Spread **19**. Slippery **21**. Deep **23**. Cold **25**. Dead **27**. Eat **29**. Read **31**. Run

72. About a Country

ACROSS: 1. Treaty **6**. Law **7**. Border **10**. Export **11**. Army **12**. Tariff **13**. Language **14**. Embassy **15**. Police **16**. Judge **21**. Passport **24**. Import **26**. Nationality **27**. Citizen **28**. Navy **29**. Trade

DOWN: 2. Territory **3**. Government **4**. Alliance **5**. Firefighters **8**. Capital **9**. Visa **15**. President **17**. Diplomat **18**. Population **19**. Patriot **20**. Immigrant **22**. Court **23**. Air force **25**. Tax

73. Verb Collocations 3

ACROSS: 1. Put **3**. Fail **4**. Go **6**. Make **7**. Say **8**. Pass **9**. Keep **11**. Throw **12**. Buy **13**. Commit **16**. Carry **19**. Follow **20**. Spread **23**. Take **24**. Stand **25**. See **26**. Lose **28**. Save

DOWN: 1. Play **2**. Break **4**. Give **5**. Catch **6**. Miss **7**. Shoot **8**. Place **10**. Pay **11**. Touch **14**. Tell **15**. Drop **17**. Look **18**. Cause **19**. Find **21**. Raise **22**. Burst **23**. Talk **27**. Speak

74. The Economy

ACROSS: 1. Tariff **3**. Demand **6**. Factory **8**. Export **13**. Booming **14**. Loss **15**. Agriculture **19**. Inflation **22**. Mining **23**. Tax **24**. Free **27**. Raw **28**. Exchange **29**. Strike **30**. Goods

DOWN: 2. Import **4**. Monopoly **5**. Unemployment **7**. Consumer **9**. Profit **10**. Recession **11**. Capital **12**. Debt **14**. Loan **16**. Income **17**. Union **18**. Currency **20**. Finished **21**. Interest **25**. Bank **26**. Wage

75. Name the Category 2

ACROSS: 1. Mountain **2**. Meat **4**. Musician **7**. Sense **9**. Amphibian **10**. Tree **11**. Ruler **15**. Nut **16**. Game **17**. Direction **21**. Tool **24**. Language **25**. Furniture **26**. Number **27**. Metal **28**. Ocean **29**. Novel **30**. Month

DOWN: 1. Mammal **2**. Monster **3**. Reptile **5**. Spice **6**. Continent **8**. Noble **12**. River **13**. Planet **14**. Media **18**. Color **19**. Organ **20**. Vegetable **22**. Landform **23**. City **25**. Flower

76. Family

ACROSS: 3. Mom **4**. Generation **6**. Father **9**. Aunt **10**. Cousin **12**. Grandpa **14**. In-laws **17**. Extended **19**. Son **21**. Relative **22**. Daughter **24**. Grandchild **25**. Brother

DOWN: 1. Wife **2**. Parents **3**. Mother **4**. Grandfather **5**. Orphan **7**. Adopt **8**. Husband **11**. Grandmother **12**. Grandma **13**. Spouse **15**. Sister **16**. Wedding **18**. Great **20**. Nuclear **22**. Dad **23**. Uncle

77. Relative Hodgepodge 1

ACROSS: 1. Evening **4**. Officer **8**. Web **9**. Deck **11**. Seed **13**. Court **14**. Filter **15**. Road **16**. Pig **19**. Sofa **21**. Picture **22**. Camera **24**. Police station **26**. Valentine's **28**. Bee **29**. TV **30**. Reporter **33**. Actor **34**. Mall **36**. Ear **37**. Chicken **38**. Teeth

DOWN: 2. Eye **3**. Nose **4**. Owl **5**. Fin **6**. Construction **7**. Bed **8**. Wolf **10**. Christmas **12**. Eraser **13**. Chef **16**. Pot **17**. Gorilla **18**. Bicycle **20**. Apartment **23**. Telephone **25**. Tailor **26**. Vet **27**. Needle **31**. Radio **32**. Root **35**. Ant

78. Plants and Trees

ACROSS: 2. Garden **5**. Bee **7**. Thorn **8**. Flower **10**. Soil **11**. Rose **14**. Maple **16**. Cactus **19**. Hose **20**. Sunlight **21**. Root **22**. Cone **24**. Needles **25**. Pine **26**. Wood **28**. Vine

DOWN: 1. Leaf **3**. Acorn **4**. Nut **5**. Bud **6**. Fruit **9**. Sprout **10**. Stem **12**. Blossom **13**. Grass **15**. Pollen **17**. Autumn **18**. Shovel **19**. Harvest **22**. Crops **23**. Weed **26**. Water **27**. Oak

79. Idioms 2

ACROSS: 3. Warts **5**. Way **7**. Memory **8**. Shoulder **10**. Nail **12**. Boat **14**. Call **15**. Weight **16**. Thin **18**. Ear **19**. Weather **20**. Temper **22**. Gun **24**. Up **25**. Storm **26**. Bite **27**. Brain

DOWN: 1. Eye **2**. Book **3**. Ways **4**. Shot **5**. Wolf **6**. Wrist **7**. Make **9**. Bullet **10**. Nowhere **11**. Leg **12**. Bottom **13**. Iceberg **17**. Ice **20**. Thumb **21**. Profile **23**. Nothing

80. Recreation and Leisure

ACROSS: 3. Catch **7**. Off **8**. Draw **9**. Scuba **11**. Watch **13**. Model **15**. Collection **16**. Piano **17**. Camping **19**. Hiking **26**. Baseball **28**. Skiing **30**. Tennis **31**. Bowling

DOWN: 1. Surfing **2**. Cards **3**. Chess **4**. Photography **5**. Beach **6**. Vacation **10**. Badminton **12**. Cycling **13**. Music **14**. Dancing **18**. Puzzle **20**. Garden **21**. Read **22**. Walk **23**. Fishing **24**. Paint **25**. Skating **27**. Swim **29**. Guitar

81. Reasons to Do Something 2

ACROSS: 1. Watch **2**. Sweater **5**. Ladder **7**. Volume **9**. Cloth **11**. Worm **12**. Alarm **13**. Bike **15**. Window **16**. Gym **19**. Credit card **20**. Hose **22**. Red **23**. Door **25**. Police **26**. Blue **27**. Detergent **29**. Helmet **30**. Tissue **31**. Line

DOWN: 1. Wallet **3**. ATM **4**. Plumber **6**. Dictionary **8**. Library **10**. Hand **13**. Brush **14**. Folder **17**. Medicine **18**. Post office **21**. Job **23**. Dentist **24**. Muscles **27**. Diet **28**. E-mail

82. Personalities

ACROSS: 1. Polite **4**. Wise **6**. Hardworking **9**. Neat **12**. Courageous **13**. Messy **17**. Lazy **19**. Optimistic **20**. Kind **21**. Ambitious **24**. Brave **26**. Considerate **27**. Greedy **28**. Funny

DOWN: 2. Thoughtful **3**. Friendly **5**. Sociable **7**. Generous **8**. Humor **10**. Punctual **11**. Pessimistic **14**. Shy **15**. Reliable **16**. Outgoing **18**. Honest **22**. Stingy **23**. Clever **25**. Rude

83. Category Plus Letter 2

ACROSS: 1. Mars **2**. Pork **4**. Goat **6**. Circle **7**. Fish **9**. May **14**. Iguana **15**. Oak **17**. Grasshopper **22**. Gold **23**. Crow **24**. Europe **26**. Fox **28**. Train **31**. Octopus **32**. Atlantic **35**. Beef **36**. Parrot

DOWN: 1. March **2**. Pine **3**. Coffee **5**. Asia **8**. Spring **9**. Milk **10**. Yellow **11**. Lungs **12**. Tulip **13**. Rose **16**. Pig **18**. Radio **19**. Six **20**. Orange **21**. Pacific **25**. Pink **27**. Juice **28**. Thumb **29**. Apple **30**. Chair **31**. Owl **33**. Ant **34**. Tea

84. Banking and Finance

ACROSS: 1. Pay **3**. Debt **5**. Debit **7**. Income **8**. Investor **9**. Fill **11**. Teller **12**. ATM **13**. Budget **14**. Pension **17**. Cash **19**. Loan **20**. Check **24**. Profit **25**. Burn **26**. Take **27**. Coins **28**. Mortgage **29**. Payment **30**. Account **31**. Rainy

DOWN: 1. Pin **2**. Borrow **3**. Deposit **4**. Bank **6**. Insurance **10**. Lend **13**. Branch **15**. Identification **16**. Balance **18**. Interest **21**. Currency **22**. Statement **23**. Broke **28**. Money

85. Relative Hodgepodge 2

ACROSS: 3. Mechanic, **5**. Egg, **6**. Firefighter, **10**. Graduation, **11**. Teeth, **13**. Game, **14**. Lot, **15**. Handlebars, **17**. Owl, **19**. Cat, **20**. Geometry, **22**. Autumn, **24**. Army, **26**. Bracelet, **29**. Home, **31**. Reporter, **33**. Light.

DOWN: 1. Drought, **2**. Restaurant, **4**. Car, **6**. Flashlight, **7**. Finger, **8**. Hotel, **9**. Election, **12**. Hat, **16**. Broom, **18**. Lion, **19**. Cafe, **21**. Teacher, **23**. Net, **25**. Fish, **26**. Bat, **27**. Chef, **28**. Ear, **30**. Mall, **32**. TV.

86. Ancient Civilization and Early Humans

ACROSS: 1. Ancient **4**. History **6**. Alphabet **8**. Migration **9**. Eye **11**. Pottery **12**. Bronze **14**. Chariot **16**. Shaman **17**. Priest **22**. Agriculture **23**. Domestication **27**. Iron **28**. Flood **29**. Gold **30**. Fertile

DOWN: 2. Crops **3**. Pharaoh **5**. Silk **6**. Aqueduct **7**. Trade **10**. Nomad **13**. Egyptian **15**. Irrigation **16**. Surplus **18**. Scribe **19**. Artifact **20**. Writing **21**. Pyramid **24**. Stone **25**. Nile **26**. Code

87. Alliteration 2

ACROSS: 1. Below **4**. Trick **7**. Tit **8**. Creepy **9**. Ding **11**. Mountain **12**. Dozen **13**. Haunted **14**. Tick **16**. Hit **17**. Blood **18**. Love **19**. Crash **20**. Candy **21**. Firefighter **26**. Warm **27**. Pickpocket **28**. Look **29**. Penny **30**. Dime **31**. Dawn

DOWN: 1. Blind **2**. Wild **3**. Pumpkin **5**. Cut **6**. Pretty **7**. Tongue **10**. Greenhouse **11**. Matchmaker **12**. Down **13**. Hold **15**. Cheddar **21**. Fossil **22**. Railroad **23**. Fish **24**. Helping **25**. Copycat **26**. Wicked

88. Raw Materials and Natural Resources

ACROSS: 4. Wood **5**. Solar **6**. Grapes **7**. Bronze **9**. Silver **11**. Dye **12**. Coal **13**. Plastic **17**. Ingredient **19**. Natural **20**. Oil **21**. Dam **23**. Farmer **26**. Mine **27**. Factory **28**. Rubber **29**. Leather

DOWN: 1. Glass **2**. Copper **3**. Iron **4**. Wool **6**. Generate **8**. Raw **10**. Rancher **12**. Cotton **13**. Power plant **14**. Stone **15**. Metal **16**. Brick **18**. Gold **20**. Ore **22**. Miner **24**. Marble **25**. Steel **26**. Milk

89. Phrasal Verbs 2: Context Plus Collocation

ACROSS: 1. Run **3**. Log **5**. Sit **7**. Step **9**. Cut **10**. Hit **12**. Set **13**. Cross **15**. Think **17**. Turn **18**. Bring **19**. Put **21**. Kick **23**. End **25**. Stay

DOWN: 1. Root **2**. Catch **3**. Let **4**. Go **5**. Stick **6**. Throw **8**. Part **11**. Stand **14**. Stop **16**. Hand **18**. Break **20**. Try **22**. Check **24**. Do **26**. Tell

90. Word Skills Hodgepodge 1

ACROSS: 1. Used **3.** Healthy **6.** Different
10. Iguana **11.** Answer **12.** Bat **15.** Thin
16. Jupiter **17.** Like **19.** Near **21.** Pine
23. Strawberry **25.** Help **28.** Generous
29. Smart **30.** Ant **32.** Dangerous **34.** Asia
35. Noisy **36.** Pig **37.** Expensive **38.** Enemy
39. Raw

DOWN: 1. Understand **2.** Die **3.** Hot **4.** Arid
5. Thumb **7.** Fix **8.** Run **9.** Newspaper
13. Talk **14.** Remember **18.** End **20.** Bus
22. Grasshopper **24.** Tug **26.** Put away
27. Lungs **29.** Strange **31.** Raise **32.** Damp
33. Go

91. Metalanguage: Irregular Forms

ACROSS: 2. Won **3.** These **5.** Bitten **8.** Stood
9. Threw **10.** Feet **12.** Swollen **13.** Heard
14. Rung **17.** Children **21.** Understood
23. Dug **24.** Hidden **26.** Least **27.** Made
29. Slept **31.** Spoken **33.** Ate **34.** Written
35. Taken

DOWN: 1. Bit **2.** Went **4.** Shone **6.** Thrown
7. Teeth **10.** Farthest **11.** Taught **12.** Struck
15. Men **16.** Brought **18.** Worse **19.** Found
20. Fell **22.** Did **23.** Drank **25.** Drew
28. Eaten **30.** Took **31.** Saw **32.** Ran

92. Science 2

ACROSS: 4. Freeze **9.** Evolution **10.** Magma
11. Data **13.** Acceleration **16.** Filter **19.** Star
20. Repel **21.** Disprove **23.** DNA **25.** Volume
28. Circuit **31.** Attract **32.** Metal **33.** Erupt
34. Force **35.** Record

DOWN: 1. Friction **2.** Research **3.** Revolve
5. Matter **6.** Kinetic **7.** Solid **8.** Comet
12. Asteroid **14.** Liquid **15.** Axis **16.** Fossil
17. Melt **18.** Prove **22.** Insulator **24.** Heat
26. Extinct **27.** Measure **29.** Rotate
30. Theory **32.** Mass

93. Word Association 2

ACROSS: 1. Butter **3.** Socks **4.** Toe **5.** Foe
6. Arrow **8.** Key **10.** Bottom **13.** Alive
14. Paper **16.** Fork **17.** Queen **18.** Dad
20. Last **22.** Worse **23.** Stones **25.** Pineapple
27. Riches **29.** Take **30.** Earth **31.** Eggs

DOWN: 2. Treat **3.** Seek **5.** Famine **7.** White
9. End **10.** Boys **11.** Nail **12.** Carrot
15. Punishment **18.** Dawn **19.** Dogs
21. Sister **24.** Effect **25.** Place **26.** Prey
28. Cons

94. Synonyms 2

ACROSS: 1. Lucky **3.** Hate **5.** Piece **8.** Peak
9. Clean **10.** Baby **12.** Laugh **14.** Chair
17. Mistake **19.** Near **20.** Middle **21.** Damp
23. Come **24.** Push **26.** Yell **29.** Strange
32. Angry **33.** Fast **34.** Expensive **35.** Sick
36. Hurt

DOWN: 2. Crazy **4.** Trash **5.** Predict **6.** Evil
7. End **11.** Build **12.** Leap **13.** Careful
15. Attack **16.** Remember **18.** Enemy
21. Destroy **22.** Convince **25.** Tug
27. Location **28.** Whisper **29.** Suggest
30. Easy **31.** Find **33.** Fix

95. Noun Modification with Adjectives

ACROSS: 1. Blizzard **2**. Gold **4**. Bee **5**. Lemon **7**. Chili pepper **10**. Lettuce **11**. Bat **13**. Cactus **14**. Skyscraper **16**. Snake **17**. Motorcycle **18**. Octopus **21**. Legend **22**. Giant **23**. Sprint **24**. Nomad

DOWN: 1. Beach **2**. Gale **3**. Downpour **4**. Breeze **6**. Mosquito **7**. Cyclops **8**. Ice **9**. Magma **11**. Burden **12**. Marathon **13**. Carrot **15**. Glass **16**. Subway **17**. Mansion **19**. Penguin **20**. Dragon

96. Word Skills Hodgepodge 2

ACROSS: 2. Fake **3**. Build **5**. Table **7**. Healthy **8**. Straight **9**. Honest **11**. Cry **12**. Apple **14**. May **16**. Careful **19**. Convince **20**. White **22**. Europe **25**. Six **26**. New **27**. Owl **28**. Dangerous **33**. Octopus **36**. Location **37**. Talk **38**. Piece

DOWN: 1. Beef **2**. Follow **3**. Believe **4**. Lettuce **6**. Ant **8**. Strawberry **10**. Easy **11**. Circle **13**. Pick up **15**. Arid **17**. Raw **18**. Fail **21**. Early **22**. Expensive **23**. End **24**. Bad **25**. Sink **29**. Orange **30**. Short **31**. Hot **32**. Melt **34**. Oak **35**. Used

97. Noun Modification Using "With"

ACROSS: 2. Cactus **4**. Gallery **6**. Mall **7**. Jellyfish **11**. Octopus **14**. Leopard **16**. Drought **20**. Tundra **22**. Apartment **23**. Map **25**. Giraffe **26**. Rabbit **28**. Kite **29**. Snake **30**. Library

DOWN: 1. Desert **2**. Cyclops **3**. Piano **5**. Elephant **8**. Fish **9**. Spider **10**. Stool **12**. Medusa **13**. Turtle **15**. Orphan **16**. Donut **17**. Unicorn **18**. Starfish **19**. Cat **21**. Rainforest **24**. Puzzle **25**. Guitar **27**. Bird

98. Phrasal Verbs 3: Context Plus Collocation

ACROSS: 2. Get **4**. Pack **6**. Rip **8**. Turn **10**. Figure **11**. Watch **13**. Log **16**. Drop **18**. Cut **20**. Wake **21**. Stay **23**. Stick **25**. Bring **27**. Live **28**. Take

DOWN: 1. Hang **2**. Give **3**. Throw **5**. Catch **7**. Put **9**. Run **10**. Fill **12**. Cross **14**. Grow **15**. Face **17**. Lay **19**. Talk **22**. Think **23**. Set **24**. Check **26**. Go

99. Preposition Collocations

ACROSS: 1. Public **7**. Common **8**. Peace **9**. Word **11**. Yourself **15**. Sale **16**. Sea **17**. Rest **18**. Love **20**. General **21**. Tears **22**. Private **23**. Particular **24**. Accident **30**. Length **31**. Order **34**. War **35**. Ease **36**. Stock **37**. Time

DOWN: 2. Limits **3**. Heart **4**. View **5**. Hand **6**. Duty **8**. Pieces **10**. Purpose **12**. Horseback **13**. Mistake **14**. Danger **15**. Secret **19**. Result **21**. Topic **22**. Precaution **25**. Chance **26**. Debt **27**. Fire **28**. Course **29**. Work **30**. Least **32**. Day **33**. Reach

100. The Way You Say It

ACROSS: 1. Beg **4**. Criticize **7**. Answer **8**. Request **9**. Exclaim **10**. Ask **13**. Recommend **16**. Deny **18**. Summarize **19**. Refuse **21**. Rephrase **23**. Warn **25**. Lie **28**. Complain **29**. Yell

DOWN: 1. Boast **2**. Persuade **3**. Brag **5**. Threaten **6**. Repeat **11**. Whisper **12**. Gossip **14**. Order **15**. Praise **17**. Swear **20**. Explain **22**. Hint **24**. Advise **26**. Shout **27**. Reply

101. Halloween

ACROSS: 1. Vampire **4**. Mummy **7**. Broom **8**. October **11**. Coffin **13**. Haunted **14**. Lantern **15**. Clown **16**. Howl **18**. Skeleton **19**. Spooky **20**. Owl **21**. Monster **23**. Witch **25**. Bat **26**. Alien **27**. Graveyard **28**. Cackle

DOWN: 2. Pumpkin **3**. Robot **4**. Makeup **5**. Mask **6**. Ghost **7**. Black cat **9**. Hoot **10**. Spider **12**. Werewolf **13**. Headless **15**. Costume **17**. Zombie **20**. Orange **22**. Trick **24**. Candy **25**. Black

102. Thanksgiving

ACROSS: 1. Parade **2**. Corn **5**. November **10**. Give **11**. Oven **12**. Turkey **13**. Roast **14**. Feast **15**. Leftovers **18**. Grateful **20**. Squash **22**. Dinner **23**. Bake

DOWN: 1. Pumpkin **2**. Carve **3**. Celebrate **4**. Harvest **6**. Scarecrow **7**. Get **8**. Mayflower **9**. Voyage **10**. Gravy **16**. Stuffing **17**. Pilgrims **19**. Acorn **20**. Set **21**. Slice

103. St. Valentine's Day

ACROSS: 3. Movie **5**. Flowers **6**. Kiss **8**. Dance **9**. Heart **11**. Secret **14**. Fourteenth **15**. Love **16**. Candy **17**. Red **18**. Chocolates **20**. Sight **21**. Date **23**. Hug **24**. February

DOWN: 1. Mine **2**. Propose **4**. Violets **5**. Fall **7**. Sweetheart **10**. Affection **12**. Candlelight **13**. Card **17**. Roses **18**. Crush **19**. Cupid **20**. Sugar **22**. Arrow

104. New Year's Day

ACROSS: 2. Party **3**. Diet **5**. December **6**. Sing **8**. Holiday **10**. Lose **12**. Noise **14**. New **16**. Resolution **19**. Exercise **21**. Midnight **23**. Harder **24**. Countdown

DOWN: 1. Better **3**. Dress **4**. Celebrate **7**. Calendar **8**. Happy **9**. Confetti **11**. Old **13**. Stroke **15**. Together **17**. Eve **18**. January **20**. Quit **22**. Down

105. Independence Day

ACROSS: 2. Redcoats **3**. Boston **6**. Declaration **8**. Summer **11**. Constitution **12**. Anthem **14**. Banner **16**. Liberty **21**. Fireworks **22**. Fourth **24**. Republic

DOWN: 1. Loyalist **2**. Revolution **4**. Stars **5**. Patriot **6**. Democracy **7**. Colony **9**. Monarchy **10**. Blue **13**. Holiday **15**. July **17**. Taxes **18**. Freedom **19**. Thirteen **20**. Barbecue **23**. Bell

106. Veterans Day

ACROSS: 2. Guard **6.** Armed **8.** Eleventh **10.** Wounded **12.** Veteran **13.** Remember **14.** Navy **17.** Armistice **18.** Courage **19.** Memorial **21.** Served **22.** Poppy **24.** Silence **25.** War **26.** Conflict

DOWN: 1. Army **3.** Defend **4.** Battle **5.** Soldier **7.** Cemetery **9.** Sacrifice **11.** Duty **14.** November **15.** Uniform **16.** Casualty **17.** Air force **20.** Valor **23.** Peace

107. Christmas

ACROSS: 1. Icicles **4.** Elves **6.** Wise **10.** Workshop **11.** Carol **12.** Angel **14.** Manger **17.** Naughty **19.** Santa **21.** Star **23.** Frost **25.** Decoration **26.** Shepherd **28.** Bell **29.** Merry **31.** Holly **32.** Candy cane

DOWN: 2. Lights **3.** Snowman **5.** Stocking **7.** Scrooge **8.** Chimney **9.** December **13.** Present **15.** Gingerbread **16.** Coal **17.** North Pole **18.** Ho ho ho **20.** Bethlehem **21.** Sleigh **22.** Letter **24.** Snowflake **27.** Jolly **30.** Red

108. Easter

ACROSS: 2. Boiled **3.** Spring **5.** Lamb **7.** Find **10.** Dye **11.** Chocolate **13.** Chick **14.** Together **20.** Hide **21.** Happy **22.** April **23.** Bunny

DOWN: 1. Colorful **4.** Sunday **6.** March **8.** Lily **9.** Basket **10.** Decorate **12.** Hunt **15.** Egg **16.** Holiday **17.** Hop **18.** Shell **19.** Rabbit

109. St. Patrick's Day

ACROSS: 2. Slavery **3.** Irish **5.** Parade **6.** Saint **8.** Kidnapped **9.** Green **10.** Patron **12.** Cobbler **15.** Leprechaun **17.** Mischievous **18.** Emerald

DOWN: 1. Wear **2.** Shamrock **3.** Ireland **4.** Snakes **5.** Pot **7.** Seventeenth **9.** Gold **11.** Blarney **13.** Banshee **14.** Legend **15.** Luck **16.** Clover **17.** March

110. Earth Day

ACROSS: 1. Friendly **7.** Fossil **8.** Natural **9.** Protect **11.** Renewable **15.** Ride **16.** Environment **18.** Endangered **20.** Ozone **22.** Trash **24.** Reuse **25.** Landfill

DOWN: 1. Fix **2.** Ecosystem **3.** Sustainable **4.** Plant **5.** Conserve **6.** Wear **9.** Pollution **10.** Climate **12.** Greenhouse **13.** Global **14.** Litter **15.** Recycle **17.** Reduce **19.** Earth **21.** April **23.** Acid

About the Author

Chris Gunn, an ESL instructor for 17 years, teaches the general English program at Inha University, Incheon, South Korea. Gunn also does teacher training for the TESOL program and for preservice teachers in their Department of Education. His courses include Effective Communication in the Classroom for Non-native English Teachers, Academic Listening and Note-taking, and Academic and Professional English for the ESL Professional. For the past two years, he has been on the exam-making committee for the Korean National Teacher's Exam, a prestigious position as the exam determines who can work in the public education system. Gunn is the owner and chief writer for Lanternfish ESL, a website bringing printable, quality resources to teachers and parents. All three of its websites—www.bogglesworldesl.com, www.science-teachers.com, and www.littlehistorians.com—are aimed at providing teaching resources in the form of worksheets, activities, and games. Lanternfish ESL was founded and is maintained by a group of ESL teachers in Asia and North America.